EXPLORING CHESTER

Historical Strolls around the City Centre

Andrew Wild

Published by Sigma Leisure – an imprint of
Sigma Press, 1 South Oak Lane, Wilmslow, Cheshire SK9 6AR, England.

British Library Cataloguing in Publication Data
A CIP record for this book is available from the British Library.

ISBN: 1-85058-494-X

Typesetting and Design by: Sigma Press, Wilmslow, Cheshire.

Cover Design: MFP Design & Print

Cover Photographs: Left, top to bottom – The Groves; 2 Eastgate Street and 1 Bridge Street; the city walls, close to the cathedral. Right – the Eastgate clock. All photographs by the author.

Printed by: MFP Design & Print

Foreword

Chester is an ancient, walled city, with exceptional character and much charm. At its heart stands a great Cathedral which, like the city itself, proclaims a message of continuity with the past combined with a readiness to move on and progress into the next millennium.

In his latest work, Andrew Wild has written a guide for the walker who wishes to explore the history and development of Chester at leisure and in some detail, and thereby to become more fully acquainted with a fascinating variety of sites which might otherwise be missed by the interested visitor or student. A number of additional chapters provide helpful information about architectural styles and terms, and a list of the Georgian and Victorian architects and their work.

This sensitive book is the result of careful research and it will surely prove to be a most valuable resource for everyone who wishes to know more about our lovely city.

I commend it warmly.

Stephen S. Smalley
Dean of Chester

Acknowledgements

Many thanks to Christine Gibbs, Manager of Chester Cathedral Shop for her invaluable help; to John O'Neill (DSO [Leisure] Manager, Northgate Arena), W.M. Smith (Chairman, Chester Theatre Club) and Lena Shiell (Local Studies Librarian, Chester Library) for invaluable correspondence.

Test walkers: Walk 1 - David Wild, Pauline Evans & Doreen Morrison; Walk 2 - Amanda Wild, Beryl Bell & Jayne Brierley; Walks 3 & 4 - Dave & Jenny Ratcliffe; Walks 5, 6 & 7 - Amanda Wild.

Proofreading: Frank Ives, Clive Cranshaw, Nicholas Fry, Christine Gibbs and Stephen Smalley.

Thanks also to: Gyles Brandreth for such a good introduction (Boswell, indeed!); Steve Johnson for his professional loquaciousness; Steve Bell for graphical assistance; Malcolm and Beryl Bell for their continued support (and Latin translation); Graham and Diana Beech and everyone at Sigma Press; and, not least, to Amanda who makes it all worthwhile.

To my mother and my father

Introduction

by Gyles Brandreth, MP

Few cities have a history as long and as fascinating as ours. From the first century, when Chester became an important Roman fortress, to the twenty-first, when we are continuing to expand as an industrial, commercial and financial centre of excellence, Chester's role has always been one of strategic significance.

We also have an enviably long tradition of welcoming distinguished visitors – memorably, of course, King Charles I during the Civil War. The historic battle of Rowton Moor, which took place exactly three hundred and fifty years ago, was one of the notable anniversaries of 1995.

A more recent visitor was the American-born writer Henry James, who, a century ago, provided a telling description you may well recognise as you walk around this unique city:

The tortuous wall – girdle, long since snapped, of the little swollen city, half held in place by careful civic hands – wanders, in narrow file, between parapets smoothed by peaceful generations, pausing here and there for a dismantled gate or a bridged gap, with rises and drops, steps up and steps down, queer twists, queer contacts, peeps into homely streets, and under the brows of gables, views of cathedral tower and waterside fields, of huddled English town and ordered English county.

I can imagine no finer city of which to be the Member of Parliament. And none more convenient. I live in the heart of the city, not far from Town Hall and County Hall (where MPs tend to spend too much time), not far from Cathedral and Gateway Theatre (where MP's sadly don't spend enough time). The street where I live is actually featured twice in Andrew Wild's splendid book. I won't give you the precise address only because one or two of the guides who escort visitors on the 'ghost trail' around Chester have already got into the habit of pausing with their groups outside my sitting room window and haunting me and my family with good-humoured ghostly howls!

Each of Andrew Wild's walks takes in a different part of the city and one that is full of fascination. If I were to liken Chester to an individual I might choose Dr. Johnson – ancient yet modern, sane yet surprising, civilised and civilising. And, in a way, Andrew Wild is Chester's Boswell. The original James Boswell visited Chester on many occasions and remarked in 1779 that 'Chester pleases my fancy more than any town I ever saw ...'. When you have tried each of the walks in this book I reckon you will feel the same.

Gyles Brandreth

Contents

Architecture

References

Location Keys

A Short History of Chester

Chester's history begins with the Romans who established a legionary fortress on the banks of the Dee in 76 AD. Its situation on the river gave rise to its Roman name of Castra Deva, the Camp on the Dee, and covered an area of almost sixty acres. The Romans had invaded Britain in 43 AD and pushed northwards. The fort at Chester was established as a defensive point against the Welsh and was used as a jumping-off point for Welsh invasions for many centuries (the other major legionary fortresses were at York and Cearleon in South Wales). The fortress settled as a town towards the end of the first century taking a rectangular plan with the four main streets (running north-south and east-west) and a surrounding wall with four main gates. Many Roman artifacts can be seen in the Grosvenor Museum. Some stone fragments have been laid out close to the City Library and in the Roman Garden, just outside Newgate. The excavated remains of the amphitheatre are said to be the largest in Britain.

The Romans withdrew from Britain at the end of the 4th century, Britain became feudal and Chester lay derelict for four hundred years. The town was once again inhabited, by the Danes, in the 9th century and was rebuilt by the Saxons in the early 10th century. Chester's modern name originated in this period. The English used the word *ceaster* (a derivative of the Latin *castra*) for any extensive Roman remains, hence Chester (and also Winchester, Gloucester and Cirencester amongst others). Little trace of this period can be seen in modern Chester. The Norman invasion started a new period in British history and Chester, like most major towns, was not unaffected.

Chester was granted the title of County Palatine in 1070 and was the last town in England to fall to William the Conqueror. Both the Abbey of St Werburgh (now Chester Cathedral) and St John the Baptist are Norman buildings on earlier foundations with unmistakeable Norman elements still to be seen. William the Conqueror created the hereditary title of Earl of Chester, granted to his nephew Hugh D'Avranches, also known as Hugh Lupus. The title reverted to the Crown in 1237. Edward I, who was himself Earl of Chester, used the city as the base of his Welsh invasions during the last half of the 13th century and, for a time, Chester was almost the country's second capital. Its port was the most important in the north-west and the city enjoyed great wealth and influence throughout the 13th and 14th centuries, largely due to foreign trade. The title of Earl of Chester is now traditionally combined with the title of Prince of Wales. Prince Charles is, therefore, the current Earl of Chester.

The Roman walls were extended and strengthened during this period and the famous Rows, where first floor shops can be reached by stairways from the street, first came into existence. These covered walkways, the origins of which are unclear, are unique to Chester. The town's position was further improved with the granting of a charter in 1506 and the creation of the diocese of Chester in 1541.

The Civil War had a great effect on Chester because the town supported the King. It was besieged between 1644 and 1646 and it was from the Phoenix Tower, at the north-east corner of the walls, that Charles I reputedly watched the defeat of the Royalist army in 1645. Chester was devastated by the ravages of the Civil War, and again by the onset of plague in 1647 when more than a fifth of the population died. One house in Chester that was spared the plague still carries the grateful inscription "God's Providence Is Mine Inheritance". Continued participation in the Irish linen trade enabled the subsequent reconstruction to take place.

Daniel Defoe visited Chester during his extensive "Tour Through the Whole Island of Great Britain" in the 1720s. "It is a very ancient city and, to this day, the buildings are very old. The best ornament of the city is that the streets are very broad and fair and run through the whole city in straight lines, crossing in the middle of the city". Defoe did not have much time for the Rows which "make the city look old and ugly". He also remarked that the local cheese was "exceedingly good".

A number of timber-framed buildings from the Jacobean Renaissance can still be seen in Chester – Bishop Lloyd's House (early 17th century), Old King's Head (1621), Tudor House (late 16th century), Stanley Palace (1591), The Falcon (1626), Nine Houses (1658), Cowper House (mid-17th century), Matthew Henry's House (1658), 22-26 Bridge Street (mid-17th century) and the Bear & Billet (1664).

2-12 Bridge Street, Chester

Chester has many Georgian buildings, testament to the city's wealth and subsequent expansion. Good transport connections were essential in Chester's development and subsequent Victorian prosperity. The Chester Canal of 1772 once again connected the city to the sea, many years after the Dee had silted and become unnavigable. Grosvenor Road and the Grosvenor Bridge, built between 1825 and 1833, opened up the western side of the city. Chester became a major railway centre very early in the transport's history. General Station, perhaps the grandest of Chester's Victorian buildings, was built in 1847-8 soon serving Birkenhead, Shrewsbury, Holyhead and Crewe.

Chester's 19th century wealth was due to its development as the county town and as a business and tourist centre. A huge amount of rebuilding took place in Chester from about 1850 onwards. Nikolaus Pevsner is quite correct when he says (in the Cheshire volume of his immense and invaluable *Buildings of England* series) that Chester is

"95% Victorian", but neglects to add the street layout of the old Roman town exists intact and is, due to an admirable pedestrianisation scheme, free of the intrusive traffic that mars other historic towns and cities. A handful of architects were responsible for much of Chester's Victorian building work and the relative age of Chester's buildings does not detract from their attraction in any way. The names of Thomas Harrison, James Harrison, Sir Arthur Blomfield, Sir George Gilbert Scott, John Douglas, T.M. Penson and Thomas Lockwood loom large in any survey of Chester's buildings.

The dukedom of Westminster was created in 1874. The first Duke of Westminster, Hugh Lupus Grosvenor (1827-1899) was succeeded by his grandson Hugh Richard Arthur Grosvenor (1879-1953). These two men sponsored many buildings in Chester and the family are commemorated on street maps by Grosvenor Street (1825-30), Grosvenor Bridge (1826-33), The Grosvenor Hotel (1863-6), Grosvenor Park (1867), the Grosvenor Museum (1885-6) and the Grosvenor Shopping Precinct (1963-5). A fine memorial to the first Duke can be seen in Grosvenor Park.

Chester has developed through the 19th and 20th centuries much like other towns of its size and importance. Only a few indifferent modern buildings mar the city inside the walls (notably the Police Headquarters of 1969, the less obtrusive Addleshaw Bell Tower of 1974 and the multi-storey car park on Pepper Street) along with the necessary blot of the inner ring road which, to its credit, successfully removes much traffic from the city centre.

Chester is now a thriving and attractive business, shopping, tourist and administration centre.

The Walks

Each of the walks in this book begins and ends at the High Cross
in the centre of Chester where the four main shopping streets
meet. Remember that a better view of the buildings included will
often be obtained from the opposite side of the road to their location
described in this book.

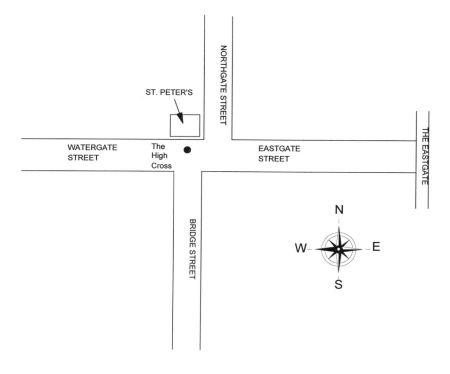

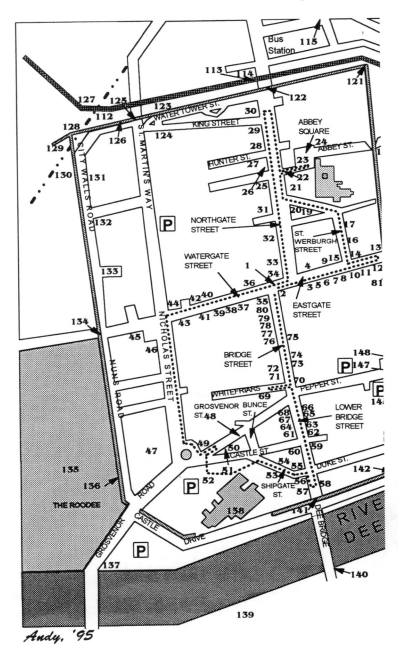

Andy, '95

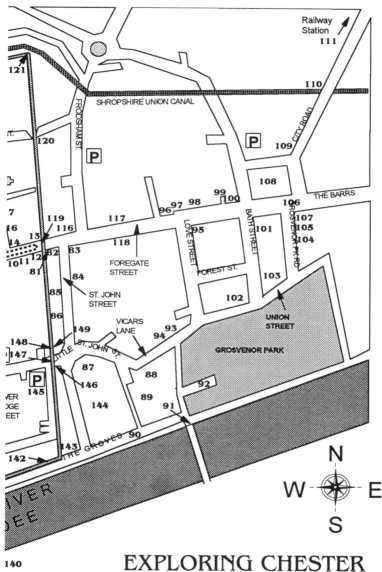

EXPLORING CHESTER
Walk 1 - Inside The Walls

Walk One

Inside The Walls

1   **THE HIGH CROSS.** This is the very centre of Chester and is
where the four Roman streets met. The sites of these
streets are where Watergate Street, Eastgate Street,
Northgate Street and Bridge Street run today. The cross
was first erected here in 1407, broken up during the Civil
War, and later re-constructed in the grounds of
Netherleigh House. It was erected in the Roman Garden
(146) outside the Newgate in 1949 and returned here in
1975.

On the corner of Eastgate Street and Bridge Street:

2   **2 EASTGATE STREET / 1 BRIDGE STREET.** Chester's most
famous features, the Rows, can be seen here. These first
floor walkways on all four of the streets that meet at the
High Cross and have been seen in Chester since at least
the 13th century. Their exact origin is unknown. Most of
the Rows in Chester (and, indeed, most of the buildings
themselves) are Victorian. On the corner of Eastgate Street
and Bridge Street is one of the city's most photographed
and picturesque buildings. It was built by Thomas
Lockwood in the Renaissance style for the Duke of
Westminster in 1888.

Walk along Eastgate Street, towards the Eastgate (with the clock). On the right, just before no. 26, is:

3   22 EASTGATE STREET. A genuine half-timbered house of 1610. Look for the date below the roof and the decorative drainpipe.

And, opposite:

4   9-13 EASTGATE STREET. Most of Eastgate is late Victorian. The black & white façades, such as this one, are mostly sham – painted boards nailed to brick. This building dates from 1900 and is a late work of Thomas Lockwood.

9-13 Eastgate Street.

Further along, on the right:

5   26 EASTGATE STREET. An 1859 restoration of an earlier building. Some 18th century parts remain. The timber here is quite evidently part of the structure of the building and not merely decorative.

Further along on the same side is Browns of Chester. The façade was built in three quite distinct sections. In order, right to left:

6   **BROWNS CRYPT BUILDINGS.** This building, in the High Victorian Gothic style, dates from 1858 and is by T.M. Penson. It looks quite out of place in this street but has a charm of its own. The 14th century medieval crypt after which the building is named is directly under the tower.

7   **BROWNS OF CHESTER (38 EASTGATE STREET).** This Classical section was built in 1828, a pleasing contrast to the more fanciful Gothic of the Crypt Buildings of only thirty years later and the ubiquitous black-and-white.

8   **BROWNS OF CHESTER (34 & 36 EASTGATE STREET).** The oldest Victorian black & white buildings on Eastgate Street, by T.M. Penson from 1856.

Opposite Browns is:

9   **25 EASTGATE STREET** from 1861.

Along from Browns towards the Eastgate is:

10   **52 EASTGATE STREET.** A recent facsimile of an 18th century black-and-white house with the legend "formerly Bolland's Confectioners".

Then, the entrance to:

11   **GROSVENOR PRECINCT,** built 1963-5.

38 Eastgate Street

And:

12 **GROSVENOR HOTEL, EASTGATE STREET.** Built by T.M. Penson in 1863-6 (although completed by others after his death), for the Marquess of Westminster on the site of the old Royal Hotel.

Opposite, by the Eastgate (119) is:

13 **MIDLAND BANK, EASTGATE STREET**, built from brick and stone in typical Victorian Gothic, complete with turrets. It dates from 1883-4 and was enlarged in 1908.

Returning towards the High Cross, on the corner of St Werburgh Street, is:

14 **BARCLAY'S BANK, EASTGATE STREET.** Stone below, black and white above. Gothic of 1895-9.

On the other corner:

15 **NATIONAL WESTMINSTER BANK, EASTGATE STREET.** Built of stone in handsome classical of 1859-61, one of the best buildings in Eastgate Street.

Turn into St Werburgh Street.

16 **ST WERBURGH STREET, EAST SIDE.** Designed and developed in the black-and-white Tudor style by John Douglas between 1895 and 1899, originally in stone but changed to timber at the insistence of the Duke of Westminster. St Werburgh Street was doubled in width when these buildings were constructed and its name was changed from St Werburgh's Lane.

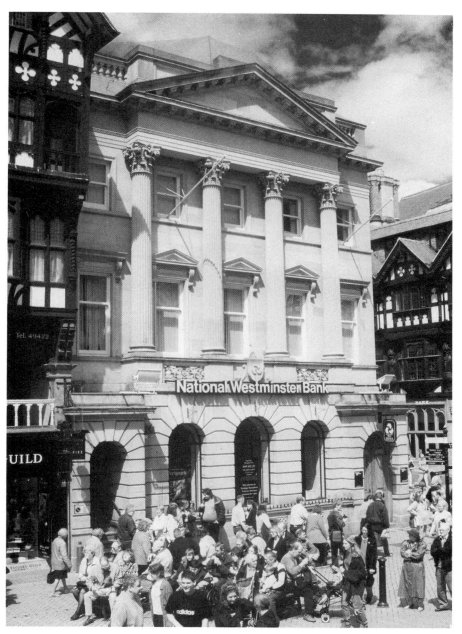

National Westminster Bank, Eastgate Street

Further along is:

17   ST OSWALD'S CHAMBERS, ST WERBURGH STREET. Also
by John Douglas.

Directly in front here is:

18   CHESTER CATHEDRAL. The Cathedral foundation dates
back to Anglo-Saxon times when it was the Abbey church
of St Werburgh. It became a Cathedral upon the creation
of the diocese of Chester during the reign of Henry VIII
and was heavily restored throughout the 19th century. Its
most famous features are the elaborate 14th century quire
stalls. The Cathedral is described in detail in Walk 4.

Along St Werburgh Street, on the left, is the former:

19   CHAPEL OF ST NICHOLAS, ST WERBURGH STREET. A
shop with Gothic front of 1854-5 by James Harrison and
late 15th century south side. This building has also been
used as a theatre, playing host to such notable actors as
Sarah Siddons, David Garrick and Grimaldi, a music hall
and cinema.

And, a little further:

20   ST WERBURGH ROW built in 1935.

At the end of St Werburgh Street, on the right, is

21   BARCLAY'S BANK, NORTHGATE STREET. Built by Sir
Arthur Blomfield as the King's School between 1875 and
1877. The school was founded by Henry VIII in 1541 and
was held in the refectory of the Cathedral for over three
hundred years. It is a stone building in the Gothic style
and is built on the site of the Bishop's Palace.

Just past here on Northgate Street is:

22 **THE ABBEY GATEWAY.** This arched gateway dates from the 14th century. The upper storey was altered in the early 19th century and was previously used as a prison. It was the main entrance to the abbey precincts and is has a splendid vaulted ceiling.

This leads to

23 **ABBEY SQUARE.** The houses on the west side (on the left as you come through the Gateway) date from the 1820s (numbers 2 & 3) and the 1780s (numbers 4-11). On the east side, opposite, numbers 13 and 14 date from 1626. The column in the centre of the square is from the former Exchange of the late 17th century. The stone flags were laid in the cobbles to assist the passage of horse-drawn carriages.

Abbey Square

In the top corner is:

24   **THE BISHOP'S HOUSE**, from the late 18th century.

Return through the Abbey Gateway. In front of you, you will see:

25   **THE TOWN HALL, NORTHGATE STREET.** Built 1864-9 by Irish architect W.H. Lynn who was also responsible for the parliament buildings in Sydney, Australia. It is red sandstone, Gothic and symmetrical with a 160 feet tower and was opened by Edward, Prince of Wales, later Edward VII. The Council Chambers were rebuilt by Thomas Lockwood in 1896-7. It contains a number of insignia from the 15th century onwards including the Chester Tapestry of 1975. The sculpture "A Celebration of Chester" by Stephen Broadbent was unveiled in 1992. A rare Victorian postbox can also be seen here by the Tourist Information Centre.

Further along, towards Northgate are:

26   **ROMAN FRAGMENTS.** This column and the few column bases were placed here in 1981.

And:

27   **CITY LIBRARY.** Converted from the Westminster Coach and Motor Works in the late 1970s. It is built in the Edwardian style with much elaborate brickwork.

Continue to:

28   **THE ODEON.** A typical cinema of the 1930s. Opposite is the Little Abbey Gateway, one of the original gates to the Abbey precincts.

The Town Hall

Roman Fragments, City Library and The Odeon

Further along is:

29   **THE PIED BULL, NORTHGATE STREET.** An 18th century front hides a much older building, with some late 16th century details still visible inside. A replica of a 1761 sign showing distances to the destinations of the coaches that departed from here is fixed to the front of the building.

Keep on to:

30   **BLUE BELL, NORTHGATE STREET.** Parts of this building date from the 11th century. It was licensed in 1494 and ceased as an inn in 1930. It is now used as a restaurant.

Just beyond here is the Northgate (122), but return along Northgate Street past the Town Hall. Here, on the right, is:

31   **SHOPPING PRECINCT & INDOOR MARKET, NORTHGATE STREET.** Built here in the early 1970s. The baroque Market Hall, built in 1863, was demolished in 1967 to make way for this development. The 500-seat Gateway Theatre is part of this complex. The precinct was redeveloped in 1994-5.

Continue along Northgate Street. As the road narrows you will see, on the right-hand side:

32   **SHOEMAKER'S ROW, NORTHGATE STREET.** Built in 1897 this ambitious Tudor style row with Gothic features (such as the oriel windows) replaced a much older row. There is a statue of Edward VII on the top corner.

Next to this:

33   **THE CITY CLUB, 1 NORTHGATE STREET.** Built of stone in the classical style, this rather plain building dates from

1808. It was designed by Thomas Harrison as the
Commercial Newsroom and Library.

On the corner is the church of St Peter:

34   ST PETER stands in the very centre of Chester on the site of
the Roman Praetorium and some Roman stonework is
incorporated in its walls. The foundation of the church
was in 907 when it was dedicated to St Peter and St Paul.
The church is, unusually, almost square in plan and was
the church of the city guilds. It is built in the Decorated
style, which dates it to the end of the 13th century
although it has been altered and restored several times,
notably the east side in 1440 and the south side (by
Thomas Harrison) in 1803. The west tower once carried a
spire. The medieval spire was replaced in 1762 and
permanently removed in 1783. There is a mid-15th
century brass inside. The oak roof of the north aisle is also
15th century and the galleries were added to contain more
churchgoers in 1637.

*On the corner of Watergate Street and Bridge Street can be
seen:*

35   2-4 BRIDGE STREET. Designed by Thomas Lockwood for the
Duke of Westminster and built in 1892 in a combination
of half-timbered and brick.

*Walk along Watergate Street. Almost immediately on your
right is:*

36   DEVA HOTEL [YE OLDE DEVA], 4 WATERGATE STREET.
This building has an 18th century brick front with
Elizabethan and Jacobean interior details.

Further along on the left you will see:

37   GOD'S PROVIDENCE HOUSE, 9 WATERGATE STREET.
Dating from 1652 but rebuilt by James Harrison in 1862
retaining some original timbers. The famous inscription,
on one of the timbers retained from the 17th century, is
said to have been added by the owner when it was the
only house in the street to escape the plague in the late
17th century.

And next door:

38   11 WATERGATE STREET dating from 1744 with a crypt
from 1180.

A little further along, on the same side is the black-and-white:

39   LECHE HOUSE, 19 WATERGATE STREET, which is mid- to
late-16th century retaining Jacobean details with its later
Georgian sash windows looking a little out of place.

Almost opposite are:

40   BOOTH MANSIONS. 28-34 WATERGATE STREET. These
are early 18th century and built from brick with stone
dressings.

Further along, on the left:

41   BISHOP LLOYD'S HOUSE, WATERGATE STREET. 'The best
is Chester' according to Nikolaus Pevsner and it's difficult
to disagree. Bishop Lloyd's House dates from the early
17th century and has carved panels of religious subjects.
The windows, however, all date from the late 19th
century restoration by Thomas Lockwood. George Lloyd

Booth Mansions

was Bishop of Chester from 1605 to 1615. Note the crests and elaborate carving above.

And further along on the right, is

42   68 WATERGATE STREET. Early Georgian in style.

Keep on to:

43   OLD CUSTOM HOUSE INN, WATERGATE STREET, which has an asymmetrical oriel window and is from 1637 although greatly restored throughout the 20th century.

Opposite you will see

44   GUILDHALL, WATERGATE STREET. Formerly the church of Holy Trinity, designed by James Harrison and built between 1865 and 1869 replacing an earlier Norman church. There is a large collection of 18th century Civic silverwork in the Guildhall Museum. The Guildhall made of sandstone and is built on the site of the Roman west gate to the city.

Walk to the crossing of the Inner Ring Road, but don't cross over. Along Watergate Street you should see the black and white façade of:

45   STANLEY PALACE, WATERGATE STREET. This house dates from 1591 when it was built by Peter Warburton who was the MP for Chester. It was originally smaller but has been much enlarged, especially in 1700 and 1935 but has retained much of its original character. It was used for a time as the town house of the powerful Stanley family of Alderley (now Alderley Edge).

Turning left from Watergate Street from the Guildhall you will see:

46   NICHOLAS STREET. This fine terrace of brick houses dates from 1781. They were restored in 1935.

Walk along Nicholas Street. You will see ahead:

47   THE COUNTY POLICE HEADQUARTERS. This obtrusive, concrete building from 1964-7, replaced barracks on this site. It won a Civil Trust Award in 1971. The church of St Bridget stood here between 1827 and 1892, a replacement for a medieval church on Lower Bridge Street that was demolished in 1828 to make way for Grosvenor Street.

Turn left from Nicholas Street here into:

48   GROSVENOR STREET. Laid out in 1825-30 by Thomas Harrison in connection with his Grosvenor Bridge (137). This was the first street in Chester to break the medieval street plan.

Almost immediately on the left you will find:

49   ST FRANCIS, GROSVENOR STREET. Opened in 1875, it has shrines to St Francis of Assisi and to the priest of Puddington Hall who was executed in 1679.

And opposite:

50   GROSVENOR MUSEUM, GROSVENOR STREET. Designed by Thomas Lockwood in the Renaissance style, built between 1885 and 1886 and opened by the Duke of Westminster in August 1886. It houses exhibits of Roman life and includes many of the Roman objects found in Chester. There are also some reconstructed Georgian and Victorian interiors.

To the right of the museum is:

51 **VIKING RESTAURANT, GROSVENOR STREET.** Built as a bank in 1851-3 by James Harrison, it is turreted with Gothic and Tudor influences.

The Viking Restaurant

Cross to the courtyard of:

52   **THE CASTLE.** A castle was almost certainly on this site in
         Saxon times. William The Conqueror founded a castle
         here towards the end of the 11th century which became
         the seat of the Earls of Chester. Building work took place
         in the 12th and 13th centuries, chiefly by Henry III and
         his son, Edward I, as part of his offences against the
         Welsh. Very little of this medieval work can be seen,
         however, as the castle was rebuilt as Civic buildings in
         the Greek Revival style by Thomas Harrison between 1788
         and 1822. The "castle" consisted of the Gaol, Exchequer
         Court and Grand Jury Room (begun 1788), Shire Hall
         (1791-1801), barracks and armoury (1804), propylaea
         (Greek portico, 1810-1822) and the medieval Agricola's
         Tower (refaced in 1818 and sometimes called Cæcer's
         Tower) still with fragments of 14th century wall paintings
         and the beautiful little 13th century chapel of St Mary de
         Castro. James II attended Mass here during his visit to
         Chester in 1687. The Gaol was replaced by the County
         Hall between 1938 and 1957. These buildings are set
         around a large central courtyard on the site of the original
         inner bailey. The statue of Queen Victoria in the
         courtyard was added in 1903 and the equestrian statue of
         Field Marshal Viscount Combermere in Grosvenor Road
         was erected in 1865.

At the top left-hand side of the courtyard is a gate leading to:

53   **ST MARY-ON-THE-HILL (CONFERENCE & EXHIBITION
         CENTRE).** Parts of this church date from the 14th century
         but the foundation of the church is even earlier, possibly
         Norman. The interior is mostly Perpendicular but the
         arches that lead to the tower and chancel (built in 1494
         and enlarged in 1678) are earlier, evidence that much
         rebuilding has taken place over the centuries. Indeed, the
         south-east chapel of 1693 is a rebuilding of a mid-15th
         century chapel. The tomb of Thomas Gamul and his wife
         and another to Philip Gamul both date from 1616. Its

St. Mary's on The Hill

proximity to the castle meant that it was both a wealthy
and busy church – all those who died or were executed at
the castle were buried at St Mary's. It was restored by
James Harrison in 1861-2 and by J.P. Seddon in 1891-2.

Continue to:

54   ST MARY'S RECTORY. Built in the Tudor style in 1835, it is
a refacing of an older building.

*Carry on down the steep cobbled St Mary's Hill. This becomes
Shipgate Street. At the end of Shipgate Street, on the left, look
out for:*

55   SHIPGATE HOUSE, SHIPGATE STREET which is 18th
century.

On the opposite corner of Shipgate Street is:

56   EDGAR HOUSE, SHIPGATE STREET. Dating from the late
15th century, and renovated and converted from an inn
('Ye Olde Edgar') into two houses in 1895.

*Turn right into Lower Bridge Street from Shipgate Street. Here
is:*

57   THE BEAR AND BILLET, LOWER BRIDGE STREET which
was built in 1664 and restored in the 19th century. It was
the townhouse of the Earls of Shrewsbury and the official
home of the Sergeants of the Bridgegate. The folding doors
in the gable are the entrance to the house's grain store.

Here is the Bridgegate (141). Opposite the Bear and Billet is:

58   BRIDGE PLACE. A fine group of Georgian houses.

Bridge Place

Turn back up Lower Bridge Street. On the right after a little while you will see:

59   **ST OLAVE, ST OLAVE STREET.** The present building dates from the 17th century and has some medieval parts. A church has stood on this site since Norman times. It was restored by James Harrison in 1859.

And opposite, look for the oval windows of:

60   **GAMUL HOUSE, LOWER BRIDGE STREET.** Refaced at the beginning of the 18th century and hiding an almost complete Jacobean hall. Charles I stayed here during the siege of Chester. The exterior gallery is the remains of a row. It was restored from almost total dereliction in the 1970s.

Further along is:

61   **THE OLD KING'S HEAD, LOWER BRIDGE STREET.** Built in 1621 and timber-framed with an usual herringbone design on the top storey.

Across the road from here is:

62   **51 LOWER BRIDGE STREET.** Dating from the early 18th century with a flight of steps leading to the front door.

A few doors along on the same side:

63   **PARK HOUSE, LOWER BRIDGE STREET.** Built in 1715. It is Georgian in style with a Classical porch.

Opposite is:

64   **HERITAGE COURT.** A recent development, carefully retaining the 17th century frontage over the entrance archway.

Old Kings Head

Almost opposite is the black-and-white façade of:

65 **TUDOR HOUSE, LOWER BRIDGE STREET.** Reputedly the oldest house in Chester, although both the Blue Bell in Northgate Street and the Three Old Arches in Bridge Street have stronger claims. It was extensively restored c. 1907.

Further along on the same side

66 **29-31 LOWER BRIDGE STREET** dating from the early 17th century. Rows once ran through this building but they are now enclosed.

And opposite:

67 **ODDFELLOW'S HALL, LOWER BRIDGE STREET.** This early 18th century building was once called Bridge House. The shop front is a later addition.

The Falcon

Further along, on the corner of Grosvenor Street, you will find:

68   THE FALCON, LOWER BRIDGE STREET. Built in 1626
above an earlier foundation, restored c. 1886 and again in
1982. This was originally the town house of the
Grosvenors and there is a 13th century crypt. Adjacent
here was the church of St Bridget, founded in the 9th
century and taken down in 1828 in connection with the
construction of Grosvenor Street in 1825-30.

*Cross Grosvenor Street and go first left down narrow
Whitefriars. On the left just along here is:*

69   MATTHEW HENRY'S HOUSE, 1 WHITEFRIARS. Built in
1658 and home to the city's non-conformist minister after
whom it is named. It is genuinely timber-framed and the
date of construction can be seen on the left-hand gable.

Return to Bridge Street. Directly opposite you will see:

70   **CHESTER HERITAGE CENTRE.** The medieval church of St Michael was largely rebuilt by James Harrison in 1849-50. The roof of the chancel dates from 1496 and is narrower than the chancel itself. This is probably the consequence of construction work of 1678 and this followed a previous rebuilding of 1582. St Michael is built on the site of the Roman south gate to the city. It became Cheshire's first Heritage Centre in 1975 after the church was declared redundant for religious purposes in 1971. It houses exhibits about Chester's history and conservation.

Carry on along Bridge Street which continues from Lower Bridge Street. On the left is

71   **THREE OLD ARCHES**, reputedly the oldest shop frontage in England from c. 1200, although very little is original. There is an early- to mid-14th century townhouse behind.

And next door:

72   **44-6 BRIDGE STREET [OWEN OWEN]** This building has a very fine Georgian façade.

On the opposite side of Bridge Street, you will see:

73   **FEATHERS LANE.** This narrow lane once lead to the courtyard of the Feathers Hotel, Chester's most prominent 19th century coaching house which was demolished in 1866.

And, a little further along:

74   **43 BRIDGE STREET.** This very narrow building is a genuine half-timber survival of the 17th century.

St. Michael's Buildings

Further along, on the same side, is the large black-and-white frontage of:

75   ST MICHAEL'S BUILDINGS, BRIDGE STREET. Built for the Grosvenor estate in 1912, replacing a white façade from 1910 that was so much disliked by the Duke of Westminster that he ordered it to be pulled down. The arched ground floor is all that remains from this short-lived episode is this building's history. This is the entrance to St Michael's Arcade, one of Chester's earliest shopping precincts from 1910.

Opposite, on the corner, you will see the narrow:

76   40 BRIDGE STREET. Built in 1858 in a simple design by James Harrison.

And across the alley:

77 **38 BRIDGE STREET [YORKSHIRE BANK]** by Douglas & Fordham from 1897. The timber framing is obviously fake.

Continue along Bridge Street. You will pass:

78 **22-26 BRIDGE STREET.** Timber-framed (although the timbers are mostly hidden), with unusual twisted columns and balusters. It dates from the mid-17th century.

And next door:

79 **THE PLANE TREE [BURGER KING], 20 BRIDGE STREET.** Half-timbered with attractive, decorative plasterwork by Thomas Lockwood, c. 1873.

And further still, on the same side

80 **COWPER HOUSE, 12 BRIDGE STREET**, which is mid-17th century and genuine timber-framed. The windows are not original and it is dated 1664.

The High Cross is a few yards ahead. This completes the walk of the city centre.

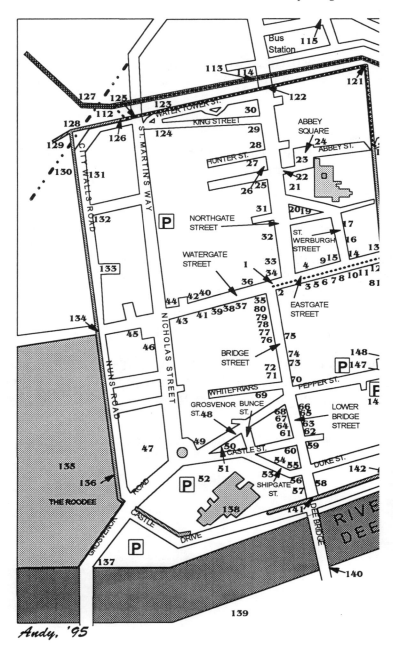

Andy, '95

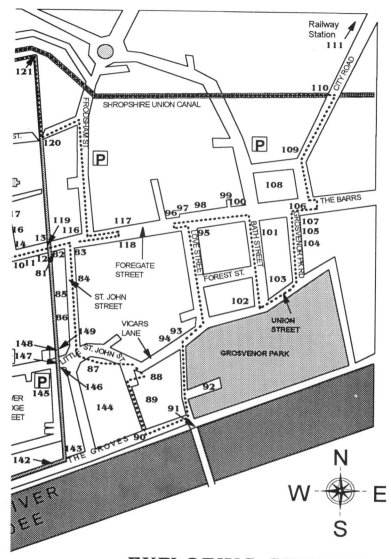

Walk Two

Outside The Walls

From the High Cross, walk along Eastgate Street and through the Eastgate (119). Immediately on the right after the gate is:

81   OLD BANK BUILDINGS, FOREGATE STREET. An asymmetrical half-timbered and turreted building projecting over the pavement on piers, built by Thomas Lockwood in 1895.

And next door:

82   LLOYD'S BANK, FOREGATE STREET. Built of stone in the Greek Revival style, a welcome contrast to the almost ubiquitous black-and-white.

And on the opposite corner, across St John Street:

83   BLOSSOMS HOTEL, FOREGATE STREET, Originally opened in 1650 but rebuilt in 1896 and 1911. The latter work aligned the building to the rest of the street. The Blossoms was the terminus of the London to Chester stage-coach.

Turn into St John Street. On the left-hand side is:

84 WELSH CHAPEL, ST JOHN STREET. Built in 1866 due to the influx of Welsh workers. It is High Victorian Gothic with a massive rose window.

Welsh Chapel, St John Street

A little further along, on the right:

85   6 ST JOHN STREET. A grand mid-18th century townhouse with classical details.

And, a few doors down:

86   METHODIST CHURCH, ST JOHN STREET. Built in 1811 by Thomas Harrison and refronted in 1906

Where St John Street meets Little St John Street is:

87   THE ROMAN AMPHITHEATRE. This is one of the largest Roman amphitheatres in Britain and could hold up to 7,000 spectators. It was built in the 1st century and was excavated in 1929.

Behind and to the left of the Roman Amphitheatre is a church. This is:

88   ST JOHN THE BAPTIST. The foundation of this church dates back to Saxon times and its history is very complex, as can be seen by looking at its almost bizarre exterior. It became a Cathedral in 1075 (the see of Coventry and Lichfield) after 17 years as a collegiate church. The church was rebuilt during this period (the massive Norman piers of the nave date from this time) with building work continuing through the 12th century. It is unusual in that it has three levels in the nave each showing an architectural development from the level below. The aisle columns are Norman, the arcaded wall passage above (triforium) is transitional from Norman to Early English and the high clerestory windows above that are 13th century Early English in style. This arrangement is typical of Cathedrals but rare in parish churches. The interior, though, is still unmistakeably Norman. The nave, crossing and first bay of the chancel date from the 11th century and the rest of the interior from the 13th century. St John's became a parish church in 1541 when the new see of Chester was created and the former Abbey of St Werburgh was dedicated as the Cathedral. The interior and the south side of the exterior was restored between 1859 and 1866 by R.C. Hussey, who was responsible for the restoration of the north side (under the patronage of the Duke of Westminster) between 1886-7. The original central tower collapsed in 1468, and was rebuilt only to fall again in 1572. Two years later the first north-east tower fell and destroyed part of the church. It was rebuilt but collapsed again in 1881 destroying the 13th century north porch. This was subsequently rebuilt the following year. Remains of this tower can still be seen near the main entrance. The current north-east tower dates from the 1886-7 rebuilding. Inside the church, there are three 14th century stone effigies, a series of monuments to the Randle Holme family from the 17th century and a medieval wall painting of St John in the north aisle. A collection of relics is displayed in the medieval chapter house crypt. The only bay of the choir that has escaped destruction is now the attractive Warburton Chapel. The aluminium figure of the Virgin in this south-east chapel was added in 1969. Chester's Victorian architects have left their mark on St John the Baptist. The east window is by T.M. Penson (1860-66), the reredos by John Douglas (1876-77) and the organ case by Thomas Lockwood (1895). The east end and part of the west end of the church fell into disuse when the church lost its collegiate status at the time of the Dissolution and is now ruinous, showing the effects of the weather on unprotected sandstone.

Take the alley at the west end of the church, between the church and the Roman Amphitheatre. Along here you will see:

89 THE HERMITAGE, THE GROVES. Tradition tells the unlikely tale that this stone anchorite cell was the retreat of Harold who survived the Battle of Hastings and lived

out his life as an exile in Chester. The conversion to a
private house took place in the early 20th century.

You come out at the River Dee. The riverside walk here is:

90   THE GROVES. Laid out in the 1880s by Alderman Charles
Brown, one of the "Browns of Chester". You can also see
The Hermitage (89) from here.

Turn left and you will see:

91   DEE SUSPENSION BRIDGE. Built in 1923, replacing another
suspension bridge on the same site from 1851.

*Follow the path to the left of the bridge and up the steps,
passing the Hermitage (89) on the left. On the right here is the
gate to:*

92   GROSVENOR PARK. Laid out in 1867 at the expense of the
Marquess of Westminster. The Shipgate, removed from
the city walls in 1830, stands here as do arches from the
ruin of St Michael (Lower Bridge Street) and the 13th
century Benedictine nunnery of St Mary which stood near
the castle. Visible from here is the Grosvenor Monument,
a statue of the Marquess of Westminster, erected by public
subscription in 1869.

*Continue away from the river. This path leads past the east
end of St John the Baptist to Vicar's Lane. Take the right-hand
fork to keep next to the park. Immediately in front of you is:*

93   GROSVENOR CLUB, VICARS LANE. Formerly the rectory of
St John's, this handsome building dates from the mid-18th
century.

Grosvenor Club, Vicars Lane

To its left, look for the red-brick of:

94   **THE FORMER ST JOHN'S SCHOOL, VICAR'S LANE.** Built in
1882-3 at the expense of the Duke of Westminster as a
girls' equivalent of the Bluecoat School (114) and typical
of buildings of that period.

*Turn right into Vicar's Lane from the path from the Groves,
then first left into Love Street. On the right along here, on the
corner of Forest Street is:*

95   **FOREST HOUSE, LOVE STREET**, of c. 1784. This is a grand
Georgian house that is in need of restoration. It once had a
courtyard directly onto Foregate Street and this, north,
face is the building's best side.

Turn left here into Foregate Street. On the right-hand side are two buildings:

96   77 FOREGATE STREET which is 17th century and timber-framed and projects over the pavement:

And a little further on:

97   71 FOREGATE STREET which is Georgian. The upper storeys project over the pavement on unusual arches.

Turn back along Foregate Street, passing the end of Love Street. On the left here is:

98   OLD QUEEN'S HEAD, dated 1508 and 1937, indicating its original date of construction and its later rebuilding.

Continue along Foregate Street. A few yards along, on the left, is the entrance to:

99   PARKER'S BUILDINGS, built in 1889-90 for retired employees of the Eaton estate using different coloured brick for decorative effect.

On the next corner is:

100   WILLIAM DEACON'S BANK [BANK OF SCOTLAND], another decorative brick building, contemporary with Parker's Buildings (1893) but now incorporated into later building work.

A little further along you should turn right into Bath Street. The buildings on the left here are:

101   BATH STREET. Designed by prominent architect John

Douglas in 1902-3. John Douglas was responsible for many other buildings in Chester.

Keep along Bath Street. At the end, turn right to see the former:

102 PUBLIC BATHS, UNION STREET. Attractively built in the Tudor style in 1900-1.

Public Baths

Turn back past the end of Bath Street and round into Grosvenor Park Road. On the left here is:

103 ST WERBURGH, GROSVENOR PARK ROAD by Edmund Kirby. Built of white stone, this large, high church was built between 1873 and 1875. The west end is later work of 1913-4. This replaced an earlier Catholic church built on Queen Street in 1799.

Opposite is a fine row of houses. They form:

104   GROSVENOR PARK ROAD, by John Douglas. A good series
of brick houses from 1879.

Grosvenor Park Road

At the end of this row is:

105   BAPTIST CHURCH, GROSVENOR PARK ROAD. By John
Douglas, 1879-80, in the Decorated style.

*Carry on to the end of Grosvenor Park Road, keeping on the
church side of the road as you round the corner. The road here
is called The Barrs.*

106   THE BARRS. This area is called The Barrs because the outer
limit of the city's medieval defences stood here. Many

buildings have been demolished in this area due the construction of the ring road at the end of the 1980s.

Cross The Barrs and look back to the corner of Grosvenor Park Road and The Barrs. Here is,

107 142 FOREGATE STREET by John Douglas, 1884. This striking brick building with its large gable is in the Flemish Renaissance style, reminiscent of buildings in Holland and Belgium.

In the centre of the traffic island is:

108 GROSVENOR COURT, built in 1989 and quite in keeping with the other buildings in this part of the city.

Keep right here into City Road. Almost immediately on the left you will see:

109 ENGLISH PRESBYTERIAN CHURCH OF WALES, CITY ROAD. Built by Welsh architect Michael Gummow in 1864-7. It is has a Classical stone front with Ionic columns and was originally built by Wesleyans who had been worshipping in a chapel in John Street since 1811 and others previous to then. City Road was built in 1864 by the four railway companies that owned the railway station to provide better access to the railway station.

Keep on along City Road to:

110 SHROPSHIRE UNION CANAL. The Chester Canal was begun in 1772. It became part of the Shropshire Union Canal in the 1830s to connect the Midlands with the Mersey ports of Liverpool and Birkenhead. It was finally linked to the Trent & Mersey Canal at Middlewich in 1833. The canal bridge was built by Chester City Council during construction of City Road in 1864.

Shropshire Union Canal

From here you will see, at the top end of City Road:

111 RAILWAY STATION. The first railway to operate to Chester
was the Chester & Birkenhead Railway which opened on
23rd September 1840. This was closely followed by the
Chester & Crewe Railway a week later. Each station
previously had their own temporary stations on Broom
Street. Several other railway companies started services
over the next few years and the need for a joint station
arose. Chester General, as it was known, was built in
1847-8 and opened on 1st August 1848 and was funded
jointly by four railway companies: Chester & Holyhead
Railway Co., Shrewsbury & Chester Railway Co., London
North Western Railway Co. (to Crewe and beyond) and
the Birkenhead, Lancashire & Cheshire Junction Railway
Co. The main station building is Italianate in style. It was
designed by railway architect Francis Thompson, who
was responsible for all of the stations between Chester
and Holyhead as well as stations for the North Midland
Railway Company (Derby to Leeds) and Eastern Counties
Railway Company (London to Cambridge). The clock

tower was moved following construction of City Road in 1864 (to enable passengers approaching the station along City Road to see the clock) and this is why it is not central to the main design. Lines to Holyhead, Wrexham, Shrewsbury and Manchester were completed by 1860 and the station was consequently extended in 1890. The Chester to Whitchurch and Chester to Mold lines closed in the 1960s and the station was refurbished between 1991 and 1993.

Join the canal here and go back under the bridge to head back towards the City Centre. Keep along the canal, passing close to the city walls and under Upper Northgate Street, until:

112 **NORTHGATE LOCKS.** Built by the famous canal engineer Thomas Telford at the junction of the Shropshire and Ellesmere canals and cut from solid sandstone. The total drop is over 30 feet.

You should have walked to the bottom of the locks to the railway bridge. Double back here (don't go back under the road bridge) and climb the path to the Inner Ring Road but don't cross the Inner Ring Road. Join the City Walls here at St Martin's Gate (125). You will have to go under the gate, which is really a footbridge, to find the steps to the Walls. Cross the Inner Ring Road on the gate and continue along the walls to the next gate, Northgate (122). Leave the walls here and go under the gate. Adjacent to the walls is the canal, and the narrow:

113 **BRIDGE OF SIGHS.** Built in 1793 to connect the former gaol (the old Northgate) with the chapel of Little St John. This section of the canal was originally part of the Roman moat around Chester.

And alongside:

114 **BLUECOAT SCHOOL, UPPER NORTHGATE STREET.** Founded by Ranulph Blandeville in 1700, this building dates from 1717. The statue of the Bluecoat boy was

Bridge of Sighs

added during restoration of 1854. It was restored in 1971 and is now used by Chester City Council. The chapel of Little St John is situated in the left-hand wing. The small cross and bell indicate its position.

Rejoin the walls, heading in the same direction. A little further along, over the walls to the left you will see:

115 NORTHGATE ARENA was built in 1976 on the site of Northgate Station. Northgate Station was opened by the Cheshire Lines Committee in 1875 for services to Manchester and closed in 1969 with services diverted to Chester General.

Continue along the walls, passing the Phoenix Tower (121) until you can see the Cathedral (18). There is a short flight of steps here leading down inside the walls (the end of Abbey Street). Turn left and go through the walls here under the tunnel-like Kaleyard Gate (120). Keep straight on down, then turn right into Frodsham Street. Where Frodsham Street joins Foregate Street, is (on the right-hand corner):

116   ROYAL BANK OF SCOTLAND, FOREGATE STREET. An ornate black & white building, constructed as late as 1921.

Turn left into Foregate Street. Along here on the left is:

117   THE FORMER OLD NAG'S HEAD, rebuilt in 1914 and restored in 1980 as part of Boots the Chemists.

The Former Old Nag's Head [Boots]

And opposite:

118   THE ROYAL OAK, FOREGATE STREET, rebuilt 1919-20, this half-timbered building was originally much older and still includes a panelled room of 1601

Turn back along Foregate Street and through the Eastgate to the High Cross.

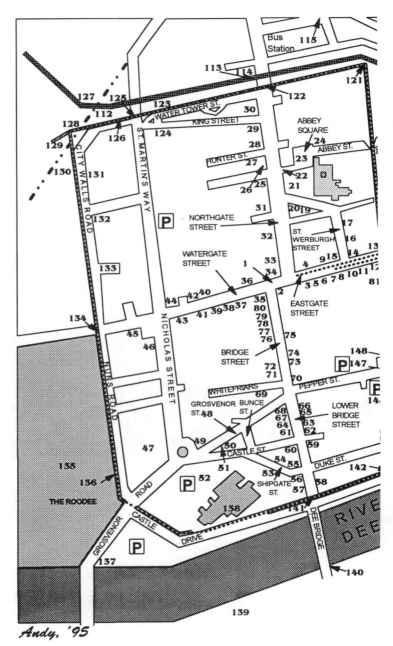

Andy, '95

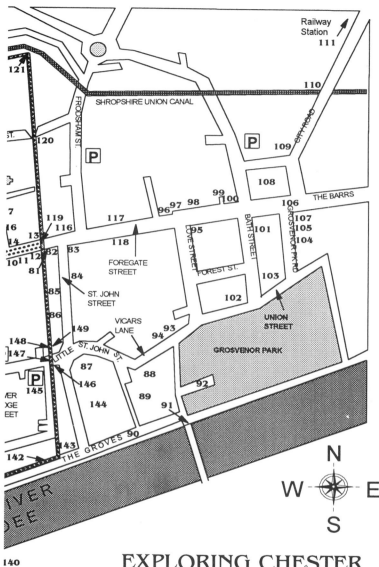

EXPLORING CHESTER
Walk 3 - Around The Walls

Walk Three

Around The Walls

"The walls ... are in very good repair, and it is a very pleasant walk round the city, upon the walls." – *Daniel Defoe in his* Tour Through The Whole Island Of Great Britain, *Volume II, June 1725*

The circumference of the walls is almost two miles and is the most complete circuit in the country, with only two short sections missing. The east and north walls, from Newgate to St Martin's Gate, are built on Roman foundations. The south and west walls were extended in the 12th century to incorporate the castle. The walls were substantially repaired following extensive damage during the Civil Wars of 1642-9 and restored during between 1701 and 1708 and throughout the 18th century when the medieval gates were removed and replaced.

From the High Cross, take Eastgate Street to

119   THE EASTGATE. The Eastgate was built in 1768-9 to replace an earlier gate that had been removed in 1706. The ironwork and the Diamond Jubilee Clock were added by John Douglas in 1897-9. The Arms of the Grosvenors can be seen on the eastern side. The Eastgate affords splendid views of both Eastgate Street and Foregate Street.

Go onto the Eastgate and stand under the clock looking back towards the High Cross. Follow the walls to your right (north, towards the Cathedral). You will see the Addleshaw Bell Tower (160) on your left, then the Cathedral (18 and Walk 4). Behind the Cathedral is the Gothic tower of the Town Hall (25). Keep to the left and take the ramp down to:

120 KALEYARD GATE. This tunnel-like opening was added in 1275 for which permission by Edward I needed to be sought. It was used by monks to pass from the Abbey to their fields outside the walls. The gate is still controlled by the Dean and Chapter of the Cathedral.

Continue along the walls. At the angle of the walls is:

121 THE PHOENIX TOWER. A plaque of a phoenix (of 1613) commemorates the use of this tower by one of the City Guilds. This tower is also known as King Charles' Tower as Charles I watched his army defeated at the Battle of Rowton Moor in 1645 during the Civil War. This tower was rebuilt and refaced in the 18th century.

As you round the corner, you are heading west. Over the wall is the Shropshire Union Canal (110) and the Northgate Arena (115). The next gate is:

122 THE NORTHGATE by Thomas Harrison, 1808-10. It was commissioned by the Duke of Westminster and is signed and dated by the architect. The Latin inscriptions on either side of the parapet read (roughly translated) "The Northgate, built by the Romans in ancient times and which became dilapidated, was restored to its original state by Robert Comes Grosvenor at his own expense in the reign of George III" and "Commenced by William Newell, 1808. Completed by Thomas Grosvenor, 1810. Thomas Harrison, Architect". The previous gate on this site was used as the town gaol until 1808 when it was moved to the site now occupied by the Queen's School (132). From here is a splendid view of the Bluecoat School (114).

Continue to:

123   MORGAN'S MOUNT. This is a look-out point named after a
commander of Charles I's defensive garrison.

Look along Pemberton Road (perpendicular to the wall) to see:

124   KING'S BUILDINGS, KING STREET. A finely-restored
Georgian terrace of 1776.

The next gate is:

125   ST MARTIN'S GATE cut through for the ring road in 1966
and designed by the City Engineer. This marks the
north-east point of the Roman walls and parts of the
original walls were excavated during the construction of
the gate.

Further along the walls is:

126   PEMBERTON'S PARLOUR (GOBLIN TOWER). Originally
circular and straddling the walls since the 13th century,
but rebuilt at the beginning of the 18th century and again
in 1894.

*From here you can see, over the walls, three canal locks.
These are the Northgate Locks (112). And behind, over the
railway:*

127   HARVEST HOUSE. This handsome, pink, 19th century
building was once the headquarters of the Shropshire
Union Railway & Canal Company. Beyond is Chester
Marina.

Pemberton's Parlour

Continue along the walls. At the top north-west corner stands:

128 BONEWALDTHORNE'S TOWER. A medieval tower built to guard the river when Chester was a port. The Dee has since silted up and is no longer navigable. A popular Camera Obscura operated here during Victorian times.

At the end of the spur is:

129 THE WATER TOWER, built in 1322 to defend the harbour. It was once surrounded by the waters of the Dee. It is 75 feet high and contains small museum of Chester's history. It was restored in 1977.

The walls have been broached here and replaced by a footbridge over:

130 RAILWAY LINE. Chester Station (111) is behind us, the other side of the city centre. This line was opened in the mid-1840s and splits at Saltney Junction, just outside Chester, for services to North Wales (Llandudno, Bangor and Holyhead) and the Marches (Wrexham and Shrewsbury).

The walls now run at the level of the appropriately named City Walls Road. On the left is:

131 THE CITY INFIRMARY, CITY WALLS ROAD dating from 1761 and much extended.

And further along, the red brick of:

132 QUEEN'S SCHOOL, CITY WALLS ROAD. Built in 1882-3 as the first Independent High School for Girls in Chester. The school occupies the site of the city gaol. The rubble from the gaol was used to construct nearby Nun's Road.

Further still, look out for:

133 STANLEY PLACE. This short street of very handsome Georgian town houses dates from 1778. The house on the corner is called Sedan House, after the unusually shaped porch that allowed the occupant to enter and exit in a sedan chair.

The next gate is:

134 THE WATERGATE, built in 1788 on the site of an older gate. The 18th century port of Chester was near here when the waters of the Dee came right up to the walls. The spire of the former church of Holy Trinity, now the Guildhall (44) can be seen along Watergate Street.

The Infirmary

The Watergate

Continuing on our circuit, You see the open area of:

135   THE ROODEE. The Roodee has been used for sports since
1540 and its most famous race, the Chester Cup, was first
run in 1824. Each circuit is slightly over one mile. The
River Dee once covered this area which has taken its
name from a stone cross (or 'rood') that stood on an island
('eye') in the centre of the river. Nun's Road was laid out
in 1901.

Look over the walls here to see:

136   ROMAN PORT. These sandstone blocks mark one of the few
surviving Roman quays in Europe.

*Carry on along the walls, passing the County Police
Headquarters (47). The walls have a short division along here
where Grosvenor Street was broken through. Looking right,
You can see the River Dee, crossed by:*

137   THE GROSVENOR BRIDGE, designed by Thomas Harrison who died before its completion. It was built 1826-33 to link the city centre with the road to Wales. It had the world's largest single masonry span when it was built (200 ft.) and charged a toll until 1885. According to architectural historian Alec Clifton-Taylor "Of all the buildings in Chester it is the one which gives most unqualified pleasure".

The buildings on the inside of the walls here form the castle (52). Continue around the south-west extent of the walls. A short stretch of the walls is missing here as you pass

138   THE COUNTY HALL. Built between 1938 and 1957 replacing the late 18th century gaol by Thomas Harrison which itself replaced part of the medieval castle. The Shipgate, now in Grosvenor Park, once stood here.

Across the Dee is the spire of

139   ST MARY'S WITHOUT THE WALLS, HANDBRIDGE. Built by the first Duke of Westminster in 1885-7, mostly in the Early English style. The entire cost of the church, rectory and school was borne by the Duke.

You will see, a little further along as you rejoin the walls:

140   THE OLD DEE BRIDGE. Dating from the late 14th century and widened in 1826. This was once the only crossing of the Dee at the extent of the river's tidal flow and replaced many earlier wooden bridges that were swept away by high tides.

And:

141   THE BRIDGEGATE built in 1782. Also seen from here are the Bear & Billet (57) and Bridge Place (58).

Further along leading down from the walls and providing access to the Groves are:

142   THE RECORDER'S STEPS. Added in 1700.

And, at the corner of the walls, a short flight leading up:

143   THE WISHING STEPS of 1785 link the south and east walls. Over the walls are The Groves (90) and the Dee Suspension Bridge (91).

A little further along, over the walls is:

144   CHADDERTON HOUSE, THE GROVES, which was built by Bishop Poploe in the mid-18th century. The canted bay is a later addition. It was the YMCA Building from 1921 until 1994 and has been redeveloped for offices.

Chadderton House

A little further along the walls on the left is:

145   NINE HOUSES, PARK STREET. These are genuine,
mid-17th century almshouses of 1658. They were restored
from almost dereliction in 1969. Six remain from the
original nine, the largest, with its quaint inscription (said
to be taken from a Roman coin found on the site), is a
later addition of 1881.

Over the opposite side of the wall is:

146   THE ROMAN GARDEN. Some of the Roman remains found
in Chester can be seen here.

The Roman Garden

The next gate is:

147   NEWGATE. Built in 1938 in connection with the ring road

proposals. From here you can see the Roman
Amphitheatre (87) and (in the opposite direction) the
church tower of Chester Heritage Centre (70).

Immediately to the north of Newgate (under the wall walk) is:

148   WOLFGATE. Built in 1760 with battlements added in 1890,
this is the oldest remaining gate in the walls.

And the three walls of:

149   THIMBLEBY'S TOWER. The truncated base of this tower
stands at the south-east extent of the Roman walls. The
tower was destroyed during the Civil War. A view of St
John's (88) is provided here.

*A little further along is the rear of St John Street Methodist
Church (86) and then You reach the Eastgate and the circuit is
complete.*

Walk Four

The Cathedral

The diocese of Chester was formed by Henry VIII in 1541 (along with Bristol, Oxford, Westminster, Peterborough and Gloucester) and the abbey of St Werburgh became Chester Cathedral. The abbey was founded by the Hugh Lupus, the first Earl of Chester, in 1092. Norman remains can still be seen. Much of the existing building dates from the Gothic period, 14th to 16th century. It was substantially damaged during the Civil War. Much of the masonry – red sandstone – has been renewed over the centuries, mostly during a series of extensive restorations in the 19th century – Thomas Harrison from 1818, R.C. Hussey from 1844, (Sir) George Gilbert Scott from 1868 and Sir Arthur Blomfield from 1882. The Cathedral is dedicated to Christ and the Blessed Virgin Mary.

Further information about the history and layout of the Cathedral can be found in the *Authorised Guide to Chester Cathedral*, available in the Cathedral Shop.

> *To reach the Cathedral from the High Cross you should walk along Eastgate Street (towards the Eastgate itself which straddles Eastgate Street and has an iron clock on it) turning almost immediately left into Northgate Street. Turn right into St Werburgh Street after about one hundred yards and the Cathedral is here in front of you.*

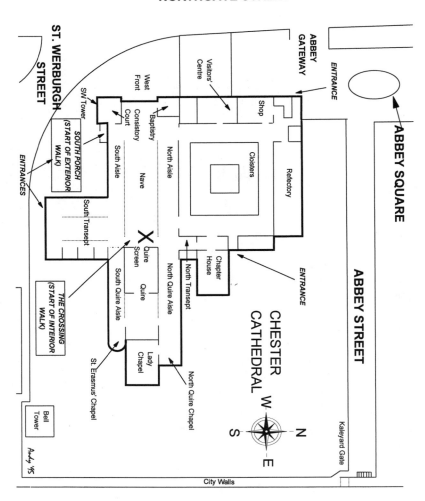

TOWN HALL   LIBRARY

NORTHGATE STREET

The Cathedral (north side)

You start by looking at the outside of the Cathedral.

Start in St Werburgh Street and go around the Cathedral in a clockwise direction.

150 **SOUTH PORCH**. This two-storey early 16th century porch was restored and partially rebuilt by George Gilbert Scott. The vaulting is by his son, George Gilbert Scott Jr.

Attached to the porch, on the corner:

151 **REMAINS OF SOUTH-WEST TOWER.** Early 16th century, restored by Scott.

Walk round to:

152 **THE WEST FRONT** with its huge Perpendicular west window.

*Go round Barclay's Bank and through the Abbey Gateway.
Follow the stone track in the cobbles keeping straight through
Abbey Square (22) past the rear of the Cathedral buildings to
Abbey Street (you will see the city walls at the end of Abbey
Street). There is a gate giving access to the Cathedral
precincts. From here you can see:*

153 THE REFECTORY, with the east window of 1913 by Sir
Giles Gilbert Scott.

And:

154 THE CHAPTER HOUSE. Rectangular and elegant, the
chapter house is recognised by the series of narrow,
pointed 'lancet' windows of the early 13th century and
still mostly original.

*Join the city walls, heading towards the east end of the
Cathedral.*

155 NORTH QUIRE. Aisle windows by R.C. Hussey, from the
mid-19th century.

156 TOWER Situated above the north-south and east-west axes,
and therefore known as a crossing tower, Chester's is 15th
century and Perpendicular in style. The corner turrets
were replaced by George Gilbert Scott in the 19th century.

At the east end of the church is:

157 THE LADY CHAPEL. The easternmost part of the Cathedral
dating from 1260-1280. The steeply pitched roof was
added by George Gilbert Scott during his restoration in
the late 19th century.

And, behind:

158　EAST WINDOW. Also by R.C. Hussey from the mid-19th century.

Above:

159　EAST END PINNACLES. These were added by George Gilbert Scott during his restoration of the 1860s.

Leave the walls by:

160　THE ADDLESHAW BELL TOWER. Designed by George Pace and completed in 1974, and opened by the Duke of Gloucester in 1975. It was the first free-standing bell tower to be built for an English Cathedral for five hundred years.

Follow the footpath along the south side. Here you can see:

161　ST ERASMUS' CHAPEL. This chapel with its tall 'candle-snuffer' roof was added by Scott during his restoration.

And:

162　THE SOUTH QUIRE. The clerestory (second level) windows are by Scott, matching the original Decorated windows, as are the late 13th century style aisle windows

Also:

163　SOUTH TRANSEPT. The south face of this transept was rebuilt by Thomas Harrison in 1818-20. The south windows are by Sir Arthur Blomfield of 1887. The clerestory (second level) windows are Perpendicular, the aisle windows are Decorated. The row of corbels depicts, amongst others, William Gladstone and Benjamin Disraeli.

And:

164   THE SOUTH NAVE. Dating from the 14th century
reconstruction of the Cathedral, this part was built c. 1360.

*This completes the circuit. You should now enter the
Cathedral though either the south porch or south transept.
Please remember that Chester Cathedral is an active church
and access is restricted during services.*

You need to go to the centre of the church – the Crossing.
This is where the north-south and east-west axes of the
church meet and is directly under the tower. If you look
along the nave here (towards the large blue West Window)
you are facing west. Through the Quire Screen is the
Quire and Altar and this is east. The organ is to the north.

The first four locations can all be seen from here.

You should be directly under the tower. Look up to:

165   THE CROSSING. This part of the Cathedral dates from early
14th century with the strengthening transverse arches
added in the 15th century. The ceiling, by George Pace,
dates from 1969.

166   THE QUIRE SCREEN. Designed by George Gilbert Scott,
1876. The Italian rood screen above was added in 1913
and was designed by Sir Giles Gilbert Scott, the elder
Scott's grandson.

167   THE NAVE. Begun in 1349, replacing the earlier Norman
nave, and not completed until over two hundred years
later. It is built in the Perpendicular style. The ceiling
vaulting is not stone but wood and the font is marble from
1697. The monuments are mostly late 17th and early 18th
century.

168 **WEST WINDOW.** This huge Perpendicular west window dates from the 15th century with glass of 1961, replacing older glass destroyed during World War II.

Pass through the screen to:

169 **THE QUIRE.** Dating from c. 1300, the transitional period between the Early English and Decorated styles. The canopied quire stalls are late 14th century and according to Paul Johnson 'the most exotic and complex set of quire stalls in the British Isles' and Nikolaus Pevsner 'one of the finest sets in the country'. The contemporary misericordes (fold-away seats) have an excellent selection of carved bases covering the usual secular, mythological and religious subjects. Two of the clerestory windows are said to be original, the others were replaced during the 19th century restoration work. The ceiling vault is by Scott and is timber, not stone. The lectern dates from the first part of the 17th century and the floor mosaic was laid in 1876. The east window stained glass is Victorian.

Leave the quire through the screen. Walk to the left into the open area of:

170 **THE SOUTH TRANSEPT.** This is the largest transept in any English Cathedral. Its great size was to compensate for a lack of building space on the north side of the Cathedral. Its size led to its use as the parish church of St Oswald until 1881. The stained glass is late Victorian. The monuments are mostly late 18th century, including one to Hugh Grosvenor, first Duke of Westminster. The Regimental Chapel of St George can be seen here on the east side, with other small chapels.

Turn back to the crossing. Between the South Transept and the Quire Screen is an iron gate. From here you can look along:

171 **SOUTH QUIRE AISLE.** Everything here is Victorian except for a late 13th century tomb-chest, a 1752 monument to

Bishop Poploe and three 17th century painted monuments. The iron gate is Spanish and dates from 1558.

At the far end of the South Quire Aisle you can see:

172 ST ERASMUS' CHAPEL. Dedicated to St Erasmus, the patron saint of seamen and created in the 19th century. This chapel is reserved for private prayer.

Beyond the Quire Screen is:

173 THE ORGAN. Positioned here by George Gilbert Scott.

Pass under the organ and turn right to head along:

174 NORTH QUIRE AISLE. The iron gate dates from 1558 and matches the one in the South Quire Aisle. The stained glass and monuments are Victorian, except for one to George Travis from 1797.

This leads to:

175 NORTH QUIRE CHAPEL. Dedicated to St Werburgh, this chapel has stained glass of 1857 and monuments to William Bispham (1685) and Bishop Graham (1867).

And:

176 THE LADY CHAPEL. The Lady Chapel, a common feature in Cathedrals, dates from c. 1260-1280 and, like the Chapter House, is Early English. It was once completely separate to the rest of the Cathedral. It was connected to the quire during a rebuilding period of the 14th and 15th centuries (evidenced by the Decorated style windows) and restored at the end of the 1960s. The shrine to St Werburgh is unique to Chester. The vaulting is original, and the stained glass is from 1859.

Return along the north quire aisle to:

177 **THE NORTH TRANSEPT.** The few visible Norman elements are here, from c. 1100. There is a round-headed arch and some blocked windows. The north door is Early English as is the trio of lancet windows in the east wall. The clerestory windows are Perpendicular with Victorian glass. The window is by George Gilbert Scott and the wooden ceiling dates from c. 1520. The monuments date from between 1784 and 1863, but are mostly early Victorian. Also here is the tiny Cobweb Picture. The original, by Lucas Cranagh I, can be seen in Innsbruck, Austria.

Continue in the same direction into:

178 **NORTH AISLE.** Completed c.1460, a hundred years after the south aisle. The wall mosaics are 1883-6.

At the far end is:

179 **THE BAPTISTRY.** Situated in the remains of the proposed north-western tower with substantial Norman remains. It was laid out in its present form in 1885.

Pass through the door at the end of the North Aisle into the cloisters.

180 **THE CLOISTERS.** The walls here date from various periods from the Norman period onwards, mostly rebuilt c. 1530. The stained glass was added between 1921 and 1927. In the garden is the bronze statue 'Water of Life' by Stephen Broadbent, dedicated in 1994.

Keep straight ahead. On the left here is:

181 **VISITORS' CENTRE & CATHEDRAL SHOP.** Situated in the early 12th century undercroft of the west range of the monks' quarters. It was used by the monks as a wine cellar.

And:

182   THE REFECTORY. A Norman building rebuilt in the late
13th century with an east window of 1913 by Sir Giles
Gilbert Scott. The hammerbeam roof is a reconstruction
from 1939. A unique feature here is the Early English
Reader's Pulpit. The King's School existed here from its
foundation by Henry VIII until the construction of its own
building, just outside the Cathedral, in 1878. It is now
used as a restaurant.

In the north cloister you will see a stone shelf. This is:

183   THE LAVATORIUM, the monks' washing place:

Keep along through the cloisters. On the east side is:

184   THE CHAPTER HOUSE. Early 13th century, used by the
monks for abbey business. A prime example of the Early
English style with typical lancet windows and good
(original) roof vaulting. The glass in the east window is
Victorian. The early Earls of Chester are buried under the
floor.

*Keep on around the cloisters to complete the circuit (you can
enter the cloister garden through the south cloister). Leave the
cloisters by the same door you entered into the west end of the
nave. Across the nave in the right-hand corner you will find:*

185   THE CONSISTORY COURT. Complete with furnishings
from the first part of the seventeenth century, sited in the
remains of the south-west tower, it is the only one
remaining in Britain.

This completes the circuit of the Cathedral.

Chester Cathedral Cloisters

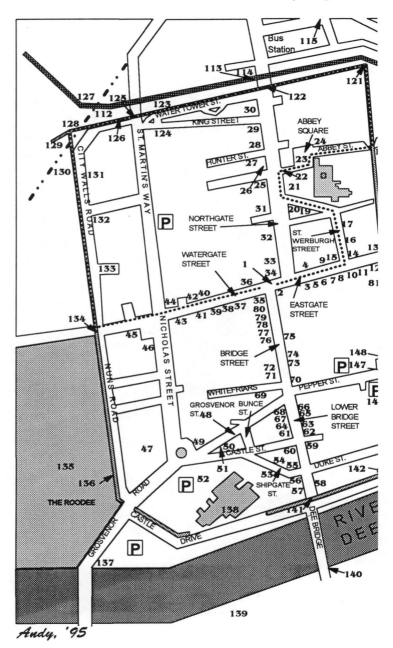

Andy, '95

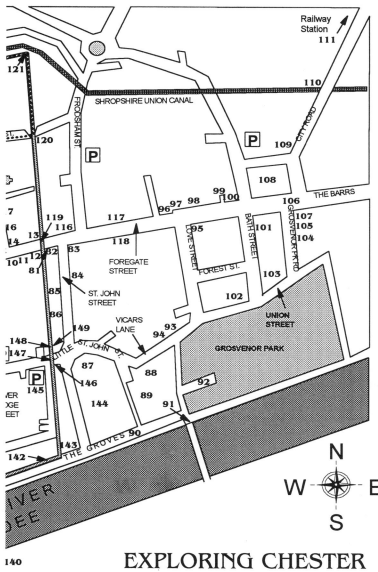

140

EXPLORING CHESTER
Walk 5 - The North Side

Walk Five

Short Walk: The North Side

1   **THE HIGH CROSS.** This is the very centre of Chester and is
where the four Roman streets met. The sites of these
streets are where Watergate Street, Eastgate Street,
Northgate Street and Bridge Street run today. The cross
was first erected here in 1407, broken up during the Civil
War, and later re-constructed in the grounds of
Netherleigh House. It was erected in the Roman Garden
(146) outside the Newgate in 1949 and returned here in
1975.

Adjacent to the High Cross is the church of St Peter:

34   **ST PETER** stands in the very centre of Chester on the site of
the Roman Praetorium and some Roman stonework is
incorporated in its walls. The foundation of the church
was in 907 when it was dedicated to St Peter and St Paul.
The church is, unusually, almost square in plan and was
the church of the city guilds. It is built in the Decorated
style, which dates it to the end of the 13th century
although it has been altered and restored several times,
notably the east side in 1440 and the south side (by
Thomas Harrison) in 1803. The west tower once carried a

spire. The medieval spire was replaced in 1762 and permanently removed in 1783. There is a mid-15th century brass inside. The oak roof of the north aisle is also 15th century and the galleries were added to contain more churchgoers in 1637.

Walk along Eastgate Street towards Eastgate (with the clock). Along here on the right, just before no. 26, is

3   22 EASTGATE STREET. A genuine half-timbered house of 1610. Look for the date below the roof and the decorative drainpipe.

And further along, on the same side, are three buildings that make up Browns of Chester.

6   BROWNS CRYPT BUILDINGS. This building, in the High Victorian Gothic style, dates from 1858 and is by T.M. Penson. It looks quite out of place in this street but has a charm of its own. The 14th century medieval crypt after which the building is named is directly under the tower.

7   BROWNS OF CHESTER (38 EASTGATE STREET). This Classical section was built in 1828, a pleasing contrast to the more fanciful Gothic of the Crypt Buildings of only thirty years later and the ubiquitous black-and-white.

8   BROWNS OF CHESTER (34 & 36 EASTGATE STREET). The oldest Victorian black & white buildings on Eastgate Street, by T.M. Penson from 1856.

Continue along Eastgate Street and then left into St Werburgh Street. On the right here:

16   ST WERBURGH STREET, EAST SIDE. Designed and developed in the black-and-white Tudor style by

Browns Crypt buildings

John Douglas between 1895 and 1899, originally in stone but changed to timber at the insistence of the Duke of Westminster. St Werburgh Street was doubled in width when these buildings were constructed and its name was changed from St Werburgh's Lane.

Further along St Werburgh Street is:

18 **CHESTER CATHEDRAL.** The Cathedral foundation dates back to Anglo-Saxon times when it was the Abbey church of St Werburgh. It became a Cathedral upon the creation of the diocese of Chester during the reign of Henry VIII and was heavily restored throughout the 19th century. Its most famous features are the elaborate 14th century choir canopies. The Cathedral is described in detail in Walk 4.

Walk round to the west end of the Cathedral. Here you will see:

21 **BARCLAY'S BANK, NORTHGATE STREET.** Built by Sir Arthur Blomfield as the King's School between 1875 and 1877. The school was founded by Henry VIII in 1541 and was held in the refectory of the Cathedral for over three hundred years. It is a stone building in the Gothic style and is built on the site of the Bishop's Palace.

And across Northgate Street:

25 **THE TOWN HALL, NORTHGATE STREET.** Built 1864-9 by Irish architect W.H. Lynn who was also responsible for the parliament buildings in Sydney, Australia. It is red sandstone, Gothic and symmetrical with a 160 feet tower and was opened by Edward, Prince of Wales, later Edward VII. The Council Chambers were rebuilt by Thomas Lockwood in 1896-7. It contains a number of insignia from the 15th century onwards including the Chester Tapestry of 1975. The sculpture "A Celebration of Chester" by Stephen Broadbent was unveiled in 1992. A

rare Victorian postbox can also be seen here by the
Tourist Information Centre.

*Turn right into Northgate Street and stop at the Abbey
Gateway which is on the right beyond Barclay's Bank.
Opposite here, to your right, is:*

27   CITY LIBRARY. Converted from the Westminster Coach and
Motor Works in the late 1970s. It is built in the Edwardian
style with much elaborate brickwork.

Pass through:

22   THE ABBEY GATEWAY. This arched gateway dates from the
14th century. The upper storey was altered in the early
19th century and was previously used as a prison. It was
the main entrance to the abbey precincts and it has a
splendid vaulted ceiling.

The Abbey Gateway

This leads to:

23   ABBEY SQUARE. The houses on the west side (on the left as you come through the Gateway) date from the 1820s (numbers 2 & 3) and the 1780s (numbers 4-11). On the east side, opposite, numbers 13 and 14 date from 1626. The column in the centre of the square is from the former Exchange of the late 17th century. The stone flags were laid in the cobbles to assist the passage of horse-drawn carriages.

Pass through Abbey Square and along Abbey Street, passing the side of the Cathedral. Join the walls here and head north (away from the Cathedral). At the corner of the walls is:

121   THE PHOENIX TOWER. A plaque of a phoenix (of 1613) commemorates the use of this tower by one of the City Guilds. This tower is also known as King Charles' Tower as Charles I watched his army defeated at the Battle of Rowton Moor in 1645 during the Civil War. This tower was rebuilt and refaced in the 18th century.

As you turn the corner, you are heading west. Over the wall after you pass the Phoenix Tower is:

115   NORTHGATE ARENA was built in 1976 on the site of
·   Northgate Station. Northgate Station was opened by the Cheshire Lines Committee in 1875 for services to Manchester and closed in 1969 with services diverted to Chester General.

And:

110   SHROPSHIRE UNION CANAL. The Chester Canal was begun in 1772. It became part of the Shropshire Union Canal in the 1830s to connect the Midlands with the Mersey ports of Liverpool and Birkenhead. It was finally

linked to the Trent & Mersey Canal at Middlewich in
1833. The canal bridge was built by Chester City Council
during construction of City Road in 1864.

A little further along is:

122 **THE NORTHGATE** by Thomas Harrison, 1808-10. It was
commissioned by the Duke of Westminster and is signed
and dated by the architect. The Latin inscriptions on
either side of the parapet read (roughly translated) "The
Northgate, built by the Romans in ancient times and
which became dilapidated, was restored to its original
state by Robert Comes Grosvenor at his own expense in
the reign of George III" and "Commenced by William
Newell, 1808. Completed by Thomas Grosvenor, 1810.
Thomas Harrison, Architect". The previous gate on this
site was used as the town gaol until 1808 when it was
moved to the site now occupied by the Queen's School
(132).

From here you can see:

114 **BLUECOAT SCHOOL, UPPER NORTHGATE STREET.**
Founded by Ranulph Blandeville in 1700, this building
dates from 1717. The statue of the Bluecoat boy was
added during restoration of 1854. It was restored in 1971
and is now used by Chester City Council. The chapel of
Little St John is situated in the left-hand wing. The small
cross and bell indicate its position.

Continue along the walls to:

123 **MORGAN'S MOUNT.** This is a look-out point named after a
commander of Charles I's defensive garrison. This marks
the north-east point of the Roman walls.

The next gate is:

125 ST MARTIN'S GATE cut through for the ring road in 1966 and designed by the City Engineer. This marks the north-east point of the Roman walls and parts of the original walls were excavated during the construction of the gate.

Further along the walls is:

126 PEMBERTON'S PARLOUR (GOBLIN TOWER). Originally circular and straddling the walls since the 13th century, but rebuilt at the beginning of the 18th century and again in 1894.

Over the wall are:

112 NORTHGATE LOCKS. Built by the famous canal engineer Thomas Telford at the junction of the Shropshire and Ellesmere canals and cut from solid sandstone. The total drop is over 30 feet.

Over the railway you will see:

127 HARVEST HOUSE. This handsome pink building is the early 19th century Harvest House, once the headquarters of the Shropshire Union Railway & Canal Company. Beyond is Chester Marina.

At the top north-west corner of the Walls stands:

128 BONEWALDTHORNE'S TOWER. A medieval tower built to guard the river when Chester was a port. The Dee has since silted up and is no longer navigable. A popular Camera Obscura operated here during Victorian times.

At the end of the spur is:

129   THE WATER TOWER, built in 1322 to defend the harbour.
It was once surrounded by the waters of the Dee. It is 75
feet high and contains small museum of Chester's history.
It was restored in 1977.

*The walls now run at the level of City Walls Road. On the left
is:*

131   THE CITY INFIRMARY, CITY WALLS ROAD dating from
1761 and much extended.

And further along, the red brick of:

132   QUEEN'S SCHOOL, CITY WALLS ROAD. Built in 1882-3 as
the first Independent High School for Girls in Chester.
The school occupies the site of the city gaol. The rubble
from the gaol was used to construct nearby Nun's Road.

Further still, look out for:

133   STANLEY PLACE. This short street of very handsome
Georgian town houses dates from 1778. On the corner is
Sedan House, so named after the unusual porch that
allowed the occupier to enter a sedan chair without
leaving cover.

The next gate is:

134   THE WATERGATE, built in 1788 on the site of an older
gate. The 18th century port of Chester was near here when
the waters of the Dee came right up to the walls.

Leave the walls here and head uphill towards the city centre. On the right before the Inner Ring Road is:

45 **STANLEY PALACE, WATERGATE STREET.** This house dates from 1591 when it was built by Peter Warburton who was the MP for Chester. It was originally smaller but has been much enlarged, especially in 1700 and 1935 but has retained much of its original character. It was used for a time as the town house of the powerful Stanley family of Alderley.

Stanley Palace

Cross the Inner Ring Road and continue along Watergate Street. On the left-hand corner is:

44 **GUILDHALL, WATERGATE STREET.** Formerly the church of Holy Trinity, designed by James Harrison and built between 1865 and 1869 replacing an earlier Norman church. There is a large collection of 18th century Civic silverwork in the Guildhall Museum. The Guildhall made of sandstone and is built on the site of the Roman west gate to the city.

Opposite here is:

43   OLD CUSTOM HOUSE INN, WATERGATE STREET, which has an asymmetrical oriel window and is from 1637 although greatly restored throughout the 20th century.

Further along Watergate Street on the right is:

41   BISHOP LLOYD'S HOUSE, WATERGATE STREET. 'The best is Chester' according to Nikolaus Pevsner and it's difficult to disagree. Bishop Lloyd's House dates from the early 17th century and has carved panels of religious subjects. The windows, however, all date from the late 19th century restoration by Thomas Lockwood. George Lloyd was Bishop of Chester from 1605 to 1615. Note the crests and elaborate carving above.

Continue to, on the right, the Black & White

39   LECHE HOUSE, 19 WATERGATE STREET. Which is mid- to late-16th century retaining Jacobean details with its later Georgian sash windows looking a little out of place.

And further along, on the same side:

38   11 WATERGATE STREET dating from 1744 with a crypt from 1180.

And next door:

37 GOD'S PROVIDENCE HOUSE, 9 WATERGATE STREET.
Dating from 1652 but rebuilt by James Harrison in 1862
retaining some original timbers. The famous inscription,
on one of the timbers retained from the 17th century, is
said to have been added by the owner when it was the
only house in the street to escape the plague in the late
17th century.

God's Providence House

Continue along Watergate Street back to the High Cross.

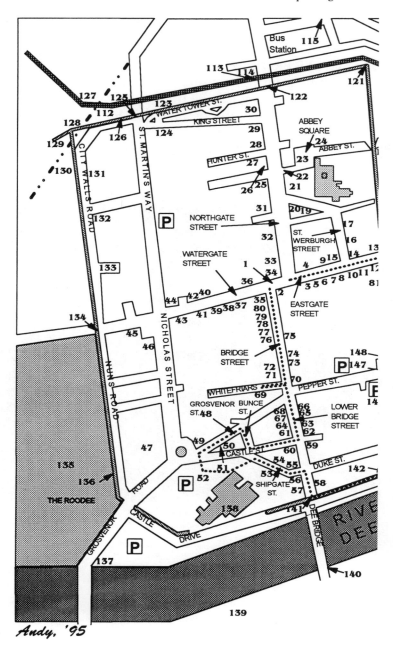

Andy, '95

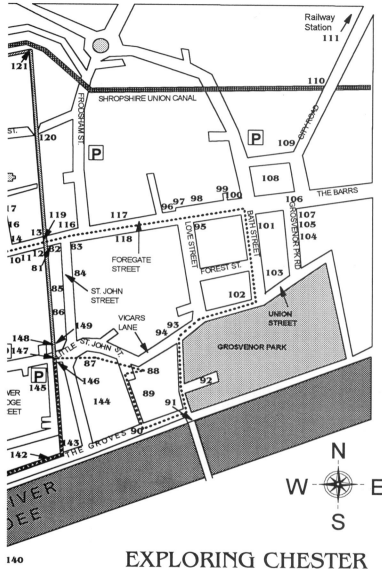

EXPLORING CHESTER
Walk 6 - The South Side

Walk Six

Short Walk: The South Side

*Start from the High Cross and head south along Bridge Street
away from St Peter's. On the right along here is:*

80   COWPER HOUSE, 12 BRIDGE STREET, which is mid-17th
century and genuine timber-framed. The windows are not
original and it is dated 1664.

*A little further along, on the left you will see the large,
imposing black-and-white:*

75   ST MICHAEL'S BUILDINGS, BRIDGE STREET. Built for the
Grosvenor estate in 1912, replacing a white façade from
1910 that was so much disliked by the Duke of
Westminster that he ordered it to be pulled down. The
arched ground floor is all that remains from this
short-lived episode is this building's history. This is the
entrance to St Michael's Arcade, one of Chester's earliest
shopping precincts from 1910.

And on the same side:

74 **43 BRIDGE STREET.** This very narrow building is a genuine half-timber survival of the 17th century.

Further along on the opposite side:

72 **44-6 BRIDGE STREET [Owen Owen]** This building has a very fine Georgian façade.

And, next door:

71 **THREE OLD ARCHES**, reputedly the oldest shop frontage in England from c. 1200, although very little is original. There is an early-mid 14th century townhouse behind.

Turn the corner to the right after Three Old Arches into Whitefriars. Just along here is:

69 **MATTHEW HENRY'S HOUSE, 1 WHITEFRIARS.** Built in 1658 and home to the city's non-conformist minister after whom it is named. It is genuinely timber-framed and the date of construction can be seen on the left-hand gable.

On the corner of Bridge Street and Pepper Street is:

70 **CHESTER HERITAGE CENTRE.** The medieval church of St Michael was largely rebuilt by James Harrison in 1849-50. The roof of the chancel dates from 1496 and is narrower than the chancel itself. This is probably the consequence of construction work of 1678 and this followed a previous rebuilding of 1582. St Michael is built on the site of the Roman south gate to the city. It became Cheshire's first Heritage Centre in 1975 after the church was declared redundant for religious purposes in 1971. It houses exhibits about Chester's history and conservation.

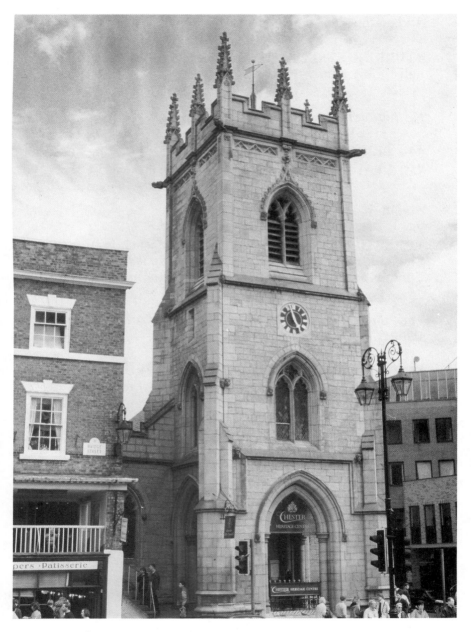

Chester Heritage Centre

Bridge Street becomes Lower Bridge Street across the road junction. The first building on Lower Bridge Street (on the corner of Grosvenor Street) is:

68   **THE FALCON, LOWER BRIDGE STREET.** Built in 1626 above an earlier foundation, restored c. 1886 and again in 1982. This was originally the town house of the Grosvenors and there is a 13th century crypt. Adjacent here was the church of St Bridget, founded in the 9th century and taken down in 1828 in connection with the construction of Grosvenor Street in 1825-30.

Three doors down is the impressive:

67   **ODDFELLOW'S HALL, LOWER BRIDGE STREET.** This early 18th century building was once called Bridge House. The shop front is a later addition.

Opposite is:

66   **29-31 LOWER BRIDGE STREET** dating from the early 17th century. Rows once ran through this building but they are now enclosed.

Further along on the same side you will see:

65   **TUDOR HOUSE, LOWER BRIDGE STREET.** Reputedly the oldest house in Chester, although both the Blue Bell in Northgate street and the Three Old Arches in Bridge Street have stronger claims. It was extensively restored c. 1907.

And, opposite:

64   **HERITAGE COURT.** A recent development, carefully retaining the 17th century frontage over the entrance archway.

A little further, on the opposite side:

63   **PARK HOUSE, LOWER BRIDGE STREET.** Built in 1715. It is
Georgian in style with a Classical porch.

Then:

59   **ST OLAVE, ST OLAVE STREET.** The present building dates
from the 17th century and has some medieval parts. A
church has stood on this site since Norman times. It was
restored by James Harrison in 1859.

On the corner of Castle Street is:

61   **THE OLD KING'S HEAD, LOWER BRIDGE STREET.** Built in
1621 and timber-framed with an usual herringbone design
on the top storey.

*Take Castle Street, then right into narrow Bunce Street
(recognisable by the stone flags set into the surface of the
road). This leads to:*

48   **GROSVENOR STREET.** Laid out in 1825-30 by Thomas
Harrison in connection with his Grosvenor Bridge (137).
This was the first street in Chester to break the medieval
street plan.

*Turn right from Bunce Street and walk along Grosvenor Street.
On the right is:*

49   **ST FRANCIS, GROSVENOR STREET.** Opened in 1875, it has
shrines to St Francis of Assisi and to the priest of
Puddington Hall who was executed in 1679.

And opposite:

50   **GROSVENOR MUSEUM, GROSVENOR STREET.** Designed
by Thomas Lockwood in the Renaissance style, built
between 1885 and 1886 and opened by the Duke of
Westminster in August 1886. It houses exhibits of Roman
life and includes many of the Roman objects found in
Chester. There are also some reconstructed Georgian and
Victorian interiors.

And next door:

51   **VIKING RESTAURANT, GROSVENOR STREET.** Built in
1851-3 by James Harrison, it is turreted with Gothic and
Tudor influences.

Continue and cross to the courtyard of:

52   **THE CASTLE.** A castle was almost certainly on this site in
Saxon times. William The Conqueror founded a castle
here towards the end of the 11th century which became
the seat of the Earls of Chester. Building work took place
in the 12th and 13th centuries, chiefly by Henry III and
his son, Edward I, as part of his offences against the
Welsh. Very little of this medieval work can be seen,
however, as the castle was rebuilt as Civic buildings in
the Greek Revival style by Thomas Harrison between 1788
and 1822. The "castle" consisted of the Gaol, Exchequer
Court and Grand Jury Room (begun 1788), Shire Hall
(1791-1801), barracks and armoury (1804), propylaea
(Greek portico, 1810-1822) and the medieval Agricola's
Tower (refaced in 1818 and sometimes called Cæcer's
Tower) still with fragments of 14th century wall paintings
and the beautiful little 13th century chapel of St Mary de
Castro. James II attended Mass here during his visit to
Chester in 1687. The Gaol was replaced by the County
Hall between 1938 and 1957. These buildings are set
around a large central courtyard on the site of the original

The Castle

inner bailey. The statue of Queen Victoria in the courtyard was added in 1903 and the equestrian statue of Field Marshal Viscount Combermere in Grosvenor Road was erected in 1865.

At the top left-hand side of the courtyard is a gate leading to:

53 **ST MARY-ON-THE-HILL (CONFERENCE & EXHIBITION CENTRE).** Parts of this church date from the 14th century but the foundation of the church is even earlier, possibly Norman. The interior is mostly Perpendicular but the arches that lead to the tower and chancel (built in 1494 and enlarged in 1678) are earlier, evidence that much rebuilding has taken place over the centuries. Indeed, the south-east chapel of 1693 is a rebuilding of a mid-15th century chapel. The tomb of Thomas Gamul and his wife and another to Philip Gamul both date from 1616. Its proximity to the castle meant that it was both a wealthy and busy church – all those who died or were executed at the castle were buried at St Mary's. It was restored by James Harrison in 1861-2 and by J.P. Seddon in 1891-2.

Continue to:

54 **ST MARY'S RECTORY.** Built in the Tudor style in 1835, it is a refacing of an older building.

Carry on down the steep cobbled St Mary's Hill. This joins Shipgate Street. On your left is:

55 **SHIPGATE HOUSE, SHIPGATE STREET**, which is a handsome mid-18th century townhouse.

On the opposite corner of Shipgate Street is:

56 **EDGAR HOUSE, SHIPGATE STREET.** Dating from the late

St Mary's Rectory

15th century, and renovated and converted from an inn ('Ye Olde Edgar') into two houses in 1895.

Turn right into Lower Bridge Street from Shipgate Street. Here is:

57   THE BEAR AND BILLET, LOWER BRIDGE STREET which was built in 1664 and restored in the 19th century. It was the townhouse of the Earls of Shrewsbury and the official home of the Sergeants of the Bridgegate. The folding doors in the gable are the entrance to the house's grain store.

Opposite the Bear and Billet is:

58   BRIDGE PLACE. A fine group of Georgian houses.

Go under the Bridgegate and turn right, then double back onto the Bridgegate itself.

141 **THE BRIDGEGATE** was built in 1782.

From here you can see:

140 **THE OLD DEE BRIDGE.** Dating from the late 14th century and widened in 1826. This was once the only crossing of the Dee at the extent of the river's tidal flow and replaced many earlier wooden bridges that were swept away by high tides.

Continue along the walls until you reach, on the outside of the walls:

146 **THE ROMAN GARDEN.** Some of the Roman remains found in Chester can be seen here.

On the opposite side of the wall is:

145 **NINE HOUSES, PARK STREET.** These are genuine, mid-17th century almshouses of 1658. They were restored from almost dereliction in 1969. Six remain from the original nine, the largest, with its quaint inscription (said to be taken from a Roman coin found on the site), is a later addition of 1881.

The next gate is:

147 **NEWGATE.** Built in 1938 in connection with the ring road proposals. From here you can see the Roman Amphitheatre (87) and (in the opposite direction) the tower of Chester Heritage Centre (70).

Leave the walls here and pass under the Newgate. A little further along on the right is:

87   THE ROMAN AMPHITHEATRE. This is one of the largest Roman amphitheatres in Britain and could hold up to 7,000 spectators. It was built in the 1st century and was excavated in 1929.

Beyond the Roman Amphitheatre on the right is a church. This is:

88   ST JOHN THE BAPTIST. The foundation of this church dates back to Saxon times and its history is very complex, as can be seen by looking at its almost bizarre exterior. It became a Cathedral in 1075 (the see of Coventry and Lichfield) after 17 years as a collegiate church. The church was rebuilt during this period (the massive Norman piers of the nave date from this time) with building work continuing through the 12th century. It is unusual in that it has three levels in the nave each showing an architectural development from the level below. The aisle columns are Norman, the arcaded wall passage above (triforium) is transitional from Norman to Early English and the high clerestory windows above that are 13th century Early English in style. This arrangement is typical of Cathedrals but rare in parish churches. The interior, though, is still unmistakeably Norman. The nave, crossing and first bay of the chancel date from the 11th century and the rest of the interior from the 13th century. St John's became a parish church in 1541 when the new see of Chester was created and the former Abbey of St Werburgh was dedicated as the Cathedral. The interior and the south side of the exterior was restored between 1859 and 1866 by R.C. Hussey, who was responsible for the restoration of the north side (under the patronage of the Duke of Westminster) between 1886-7. The original central tower collapsed in 1468, and was rebuilt only to fall again in 1572. Two years later the first north-east tower fell and destroyed part of the church. It was rebuilt but collapsed again in 1881 destroying the 13th century north porch. This was subsequently rebuilt the following year. Remains of this tower can still be seen near the main entrance. The current north-east tower dates from the 1886-7 rebuilding. Inside the church, there are three 14th century stone effigies, a series of monuments to the Randle Holme family from the 17th century and a medieval wall painting of St John in the north aisle. A collection of relics is displayed in the medieval chapter house crypt. The only bay of the choir that has escaped destruction is now the attractive Warburton Chapel. The aluminium figure of the Virgin in this south-east chapel was added in 1969. Chester's Victorian architects have left their mark on St John the Baptist. The east window is by T.M.. Penson (1860-66), the reredos by John Douglas (1876-77) and the organ case by Thomas Lockwood (1895). The east end and part of the west end of the church fell into disuse when the church lost its collegiate status at the time of the Dissolution and is now ruinous, showing the effects of the weather on unprotected sandstone.

Take the alley at the west end of the church (between the church and the Roman Amphitheatre). On the left at the bottom is:

89   THE HERMITAGE, THE GROVES. Tradition tells the unlikely tale that this stone cell was the retreat of Harold who survived the Battle of Hastings and lived out his life as an exile in Chester. The conversion to a private house took place in the early 20th century.

You come out at the River Dee. The riverside walk here is:

90   THE GROVES. Laid out in the 1880s by Alderman Charles Brown, one of the "Browns of Chester".

Turn left and you will see:

91   DEE SUSPENSION BRIDGE. Built in 1923, replacing another suspension bridge on the same site from 1851.

Follow the path to the left of the bridge and up the steps, passing the Hermitage on the left. On the right here is the entrance to:

92   GROSVENOR PARK. Laid out in 1867 at the expense of the Marquess of Westminster. The Shipgate, removed from the city walls in 1830, stands here as do arches from the ruin of St Michael (Lower Bridge Street) and the 13th century Benedictine nunnery of St Mary which stood near the castle. Visible from here is the Grosvenor Monument, a statue of the Marquess of Westminster, erected by public subscription in 1869.

This path leads past the east end of St John the Baptist to Vicar's Lane. Immediately in front of you is:

93   GROSVENOR CLUB, VICARS LANE. Formerly the rectory of St John's, this handsome building dates from the mid-18th century.

Turn right from the path along Vicars Lane, then second left into Bath Street.

101   BATH STREET. Designed by prominent architect John Douglas in 1902-3. John Douglas was responsible for many other buildings in Chester.

Turn left at the top of Bath Street into Foregate Street. Almost immediately on the right are:

99   PARKER'S BUILDINGS, built in 1889 for retired employees

Bath Street

of the Eaton estate using different coloured brick for
decorative effect.

Further along Foregate Street, on the same side:

98   **OLD QUEEN'S HEAD**, dated 1508 and 1937, indicating its
original date of construction and its later rebuilding.

Then:

97   **71 FOREGATE STREET** which is Georgian. The upper
storeys project over the pavement on unusual arches.

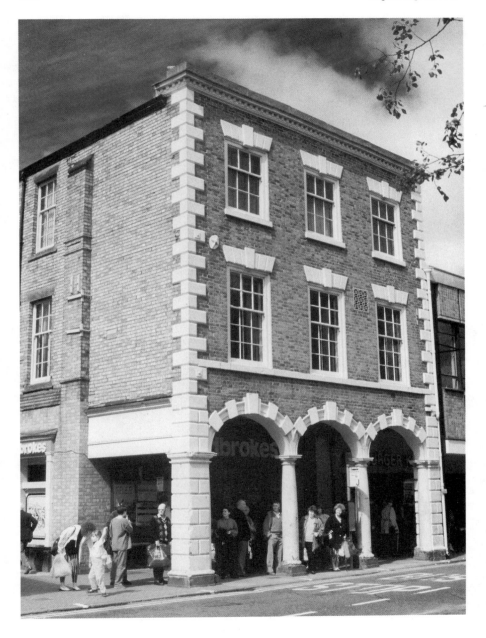

71 Foregate Street

And:

96   77 FOREGATE STREET, which is 17th century and timber-framed:

Keep on to:

117 THE FORMER OLD NAG'S HEAD, rebuilt in 1914 and restored in 1980 as part of Boot's.

And opposite:

118 THE ROYAL OAK, FOREGATE STREET, rebuilt 1919-20, this half-timbered building was originally much older and still includes a panelled room of 1601

Continue along Foregate Street. On the left, on the corner of St John Street, is:

83   BLOSSOMS HOTEL, FOREGATE STREET, Originally opened in 1650 but rebuilt in 1896 and 1911. The latter work aligned the building to the rest of the street. The Blossoms was the terminus of the London – Chester stage-coach.

Across St John Street, is

82   LLOYD'S BANK, FOREGATE STREET. Built of stone in the Greek Revival style, a welcome contrast to the almost ubiquitous black-and-white.

And next door:

81   OLD BANK BUILDINGS, FOREGATE STREET. An asymmetrical half-timbered and turreted building projecting over the pavement on piers, built by Thomas Lockwood in 1895.

Then:

119   THE EASTGATE. The Eastgate was built in 1768-9 to
replace an earlier gate that had been removed in 1706.
The ironwork and the Diamond Jubilee Clock were added
by John Douglas in 1897-9. The Arms of the Grosvenors
can be seen on the eastern side.

On the left-hand side beyond the Eastgate is:

12   GROSVENOR HOTEL, EASTGATE STREET. Built by T.M.
Penson in 1863-6 (although completed by others after his
death), for the Marquess of Westminster on the site of the
old Royal Hotel.

Continue along Eastgate Street back to the High Cross.

Walk Seven

Short Walk: The Rows

The Rows are perhaps Chester's most famous features. These first floor walkways occur on all four of the streets that meet at the High Cross and have been seen in Chester since at least the 13th century. Their exact origin is unknown. Most of the Rows in Chester (and, indeed, most of the buildings themselves) are Victorian, but walk around the Rows and you will walk through buildings from the 17th century onwards.

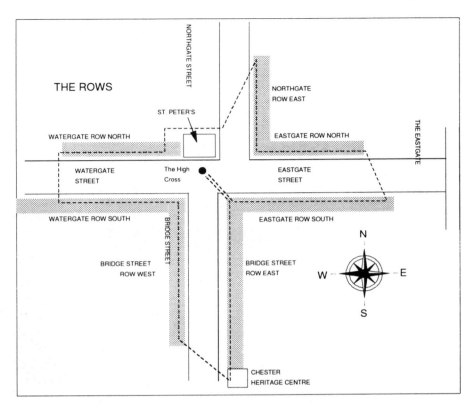

Daniel Defoe had a poor opinion of the Rows, they "make the city look old and ugly". Follow this walk to see if you agree.

The walk starts and finishes, like the others, at the High Cross.

Start from the High Cross and align yourself towards the Eastgate. Climb up the wide steps in front and to the right of you onto **EASTGATE ROW SOUTH** and head towards the Eastgate. This row ends at the entrance to the Grosvenor Precinct. Cross Eastgate Street and climb the steps next to the stone bank building to join **EASTGATE ROW NORTH**. A flight of steps leads down to Northgate Street here. Keep to the left of them and around the corner onto **NORTHGATE ROW**. Follow this to its end. Opposite here is Shoemaker's Row (not a real row). Turn left from the steps down from Northgate Row back towards the High Cross. Take the small alley on the right to St Peter's Churchyard. Pass straight through this small attractive courtyard and on to **WATERGATE ROW NORTH**. Turn right onto the Row and follow it to its end on Crook Street. Cross Watergate Street and join **WATERGATE ROW SOUTH** heading back towards the High Cross. Keep around the corner into **BRIDGE STREET ROW WEST**. Leave this Row at Pierpoint Lane (the second of the alleys crossed between the buildings). Continue along Bridge Street at street level (away from the High Cross) and cross to Chester Heritage Centre. You can join **BRIDGE STREET ROW EAST** here to head back along Bridge Street and back to our starting point.

St Peter's churchyard

The Styles of English Architecture

The vast majority of English buildings are from the Victorian era and after. The majority of those that existed before the 19th century are ecclesiastical, but many fine examples of secular buildings from Norman times onwards do exist.

Buildings can be grouped into a number of broad styles, reflecting both the tastes and engineering capabilities of the times. Dating churches, in particular, can be very hazardous due to the overlap of a number of the styles, especially between contemporary buildings in the north and south (and in town and country), and the continual rebuilding of church buildings, in part or in whole, to meet the changing needs of the ecclesiastical community. The zeal of the Victorian church builders and restorers does not aid the enthusiast of church architecture. Some would build new churches or restore old churches in the exact style of Medieval builders while others would build or restore churches in they way they think that Medieval buildings should look, not always to the buildings' advantage.

Saxon, c800 – c1100

The remaining complete Anglo-Saxon buildings are very few in number, although fragments are reasonably commonplace. Anglo-Saxon churches are characteristically small in size with thick walls and small round-arched or triangular windows. None remains in Cheshire.

Norman, c1066 – c1230

Many Norman buildings, church buildings in particular, have Saxon characteristics and there is a period of transition between the two styles as the Norman influence spread through the country. Norman churches are rectangular with apsidal chancels, becoming square after c1130. There was very little decoration until c1130 when churches began to become progressively more elaborate. Doors are small with a decorated typanium, later becoming highly decorated within multi-arched recesses. Windows are tall and round-headed.

Early English, c1190 – c1290

Early English is the first of the three Medieval church-building styles collectively known as Gothic. Churches become more rectangular in this period, apsidal chancels disappeared and new aisles and naves were often added to older buildings. The pointed arch completely replaced the rounded arch, and tall lancet windows were introduced, often in groups of three or five. Window tracery began to appear with simple piercing known as plate tracery. Spires were usually narrow and of the broach type which overhang the tower. Roofs were high pitched.

Decorated, c1290 – c1350

Elaborate window tracery gradually replaced plate tracery with geometric designs (earlier) and free-flowing curvilinear designs (later). Windows became bigger. The bases of spires began to recede from the edges of towers and eventually to disappear behind parapets. There was increased use of ornamental masonry.

Perpendicular, c1350 – c1550

Perpendicular churches are instantly recognisable by the shape and style of their windows. The window arches are lower and less pointed than previous styles with the emphasis on rectilinear tracery. West towers (usually without spires) are tall and often with elaborate ornamental masonry. Low pitched roofs with crocketed pinnacles and battlements are common.

Renaissance (Elizabethan & Jacobean), c1530 – c1670

Large Elizabethan houses are generally symmetrical, E-planned, north-facing and built of stone or brick. Smaller houses were often timber-framed. Genuine "black-and-white" houses tend to date from this period.

Cowper House (1664): Renaissance style of architecture

Shipgate House (18th century): Classical style of architecture

Classical, Stuart & Georgian, c1650 – c1850

Church building stopped for the most part for many years following Henry VIII's break with Rome in the mid-sixteenth century. The taste in secular architecture changed during the Renaissance to reflect the strict building rules of the ancient Greeks and Romans. The main features of Classical architecture can be summarised in two words – order and symmetry. Greek and Roman columns and pediments are familiar components of buildings in the Classical style.

Stuart and Georgian houses are almost always symmetrical and, often, almost cubic. The most obvious visual attributes of a Georgian house are the sash windows although many of these have been altered or replaced. The Georgian terrace is still a common feature in many towns and cities.

Victorian & Edwardian, c1835 – 1914

Many Victorian churches are revivals of earlier building styles, sometimes accurate, sometimes not. Many churches of this period

The City Library (early 20th century): Victorian/Edwardian style of architecture

show a debt to the Medieval era but with a style uniquely Victorian, a sort of garish, bastardised Gothic, often known as Gothick or High Victorian.

Victorian housing is typified by the back-to-back terrace in industrial areas and the bay-windowed semi in urban areas.

Edwardian architecture is, strictly speaking, a continuation of the Victorian era, but generally less extravagant and with a penchant for decorative tiling.

Modern, c1920 to date

Modern architecture has also gone through phases, generally short, but, due to the great number of modern buildings still in existence, these phases still have a great effect on today's urban scene. The great urban building of the 1930s, 1940s and 1950s has resulted in the common sight of the semi-detached house and better class terrace. The Swiss-born architect Le Corbusier was almost single-handedly responsible for influencing the great concrete disasters of the 1960s and 1970s. The buildings of the 1980s and 1990s have been built with more traditional materials such as brick, stone and glass (with concrete or steel frames) but applied with the greater technical knowledge that the modern architect must use.

Glossary of Architectural Terms

AISLE   a walkway in a church that runs laterally through
                     the building, separated from the NAVE by an
                     ARCADE.

ARCADE   a number of arches on columns

BALUSTRADE   a series of short posts or pillars supporting a rail

BAY   the vertical division of a building into segments
                     usually denoted by windows or columns

BUTTRESS   masonry or brickwork built onto a wall to add
                     strength

CHANCEL   the part of a church used by the clergy and in
                     which the altar is placed

CHOIR   see QUIRE

CLERESTORY   the upper part of the NAVE, CHOIR/QUIRE and
                     TRANSEPTS containing a range of windows
                     immediately beneath the roof of a church

CLOISTER   an ARCADED quadrangle with buildings off

CORBEL   a block of stone projecting from a wall in
                     support of a roof, vault, parapet or other
                     feature. Often carved.

CROSSING   the part of a church where the NAVE and
                     TRANSEPTS meet

CRYPT   underground chamber, usually VAULTED

FAÇADE   the exterior face of a building

GABLE	the triangular part of wall at the end of a roof
HALF-TIMBERED	exposed timber-framing with plaster or brick infill
HAMMER-BEAM	a roof where horizontal beams projecting at right angles support the vertical members
LANCET	tall pointed window
MISERICORD(E)	a hinged wooden seat
NAVE	the part of the church used by the congregation, containing the pews
ORIEL	a type of window that projects from a building instead of being flush with it
QUIRE	(also known as *Choir*) the part of church that holds the singers and forms part of the CHANCEL
TRACERY	intersecting ornamental stonework used to decorate windows
TRANSEPT	the transverse parts of a cruciform church
TRIFORIUM	an arcaded wall passage above the AISLE of a church
VAULT	an arched roof or ceiling

Chester's Georgian and Victorian Architects

Much of Chester's present-day appearance is due to a handful of architects, often under the patronage of one of the Dukes of Westminster. These architects are listed below, together with the buildings in Chester for which they were responsible. The numbers in brackets cross-reference the entries in this book.

Thomas Harrison (1744-1829)	Chester Castle, 1788-1822 (52) St Peter's, The Cross, 1803 (34) City Club, Northgate Street, 1808 (33) Northgate, 1808-10 (122) Methodist Church, St. John Street, 1811 (86) Cathedral, from 1818 (18) Grosvenor Street, 1825-30 (48) Grosvenor Bridge, 1826-33 (137)
Sir George Gilbert Scott (1811-1878)	St Thomas of Canterbury, Parkgate Road, 1869-72 Cathedral, from 1868 (18)
James Harrison (1814-1866)	Chester Heritage Centre [St Michael], 1849-50 (70) Queen's Park, c. 1851 Viking Restaurant, Grosvenor Street, 1851-3 (51) Chapel of St Nicholas, St Werburgh Street, 1854-5 (19) 40 Bridge Street, 1858 (76) St Olave, St Olave Street, 1859 (59) St Mary-on-the-Hill, 1861-2 (53) God's Providence House, Watergate Street, 1862 (37) Guildhall [Holy Trinity], Watergate Street, 1865-9 (44)

T.M. Penson (1818-1864)	Old Cemetery, Grosvenor Road, 1848-50 34/36 Eastgate Street, 1856 (8) Brown's Crypt Buildings, 1858 (6) Queen Hotel, Station Road, 1860-1 St John Baptist, East Window, 1860-6 (88) Grosvenor Hotel, Eastgate Street, 1863-6 (12)
Sir Arthur Blomfield (1829-1899)	Barclay's [King's School], St Werburgh Street, 1875-7 (21) Cathedral, from 1882 (18)
Thomas Lockwood (1830-1900)	The Plane Tree, Bridge Street, 1873 (79) Grosvenor Museum, Grosvenor Street, 1885-6 (50) 2 Eastgate Street / 1 Bridge Street, 1888 (2) 2-4 Bridge Street, 1892 (35) St Mark, Saltney, 1892-3 William Deacon's Bank, Foregate Street, 1893 (100) Campbell Memorial Hall, Boughton, 1894-7 Old Bank Buildings, Foregate Street, 1895 (81) St John Baptist, Organ case, 1895 (88) Council Chambers, Town Hall, Northgate Street, 1896-7 (25) Bishop Lloyd's House, late 19th century (41) 9-13 Eastgate Street, 1900 (4)
John Douglas (1830-1911)	St John the Baptist, Reredos, 1876-7 (88) Christchurch, Gloucester Road, 1876-1900 St Paul, Boughton, 1876 Grosvenor Park Road, 1879 (104) Baptist Church, Grosvenor Park Road, 1879- 80 (105) Vicarage of St Thomas, Parkgate Road, 1880 Midland Bank, Eastgate Street, 1883-4 (13) 142 Foregate Street, 1884 (107) St Werburgh Street, East Side, 1895-1899 (16) 38 Bridge Street, 1897 (77) Diamond Jubilee Clock, Eastgate, 1897-9 (119) St Oswald's Chambers, St Werburgh Street, 1890s (17) Bath Street, 1902-3 (101)

Index of Locations

Houses & Shops

Hotels, Pubs & Restaurants

Banks

Streets & Squares

Religious Buildings

Gates, Towers & Steps

Cinemas & Theatres

Municipal Buildings

Historical Monuments

Museums

Waterways & Bridges

Schools

Others

Cathedral

Architecture:

Monastic:

Chapels & Baptistry:

Fixtures:

Visitors' Rooms:

Sources

Baker, S.K., *Rail Atlas of Britain*, OPC, Third Edition, 1980

Betjeman, John, *A Pictorial History of English Architecture*, Penguin, 1974

Binney, Marcus & Pearce, Edward (eds.) *Railway Architecture*, Bloomsbury, 1979

Cady, Michael (ed.), *The AA Book of Town Walks in Britain*, Automobile Association, 1984

Cheshire County Council Heritage & Recreation Service, *Discovering Cheshire Churches*, Cheshire County Council, 1989

Clifton-Taylor, Alec, *The Cathedrals of England*, Thames & Hudson, 1967

Clifton-Taylor, Alec, *English Parish Churches as Works of Art*, Batsford, 1974

Clifton-Taylor, Alec, *Buildings of Delight*, Gollancz, 1986

Council of the City of Chester / Chester Society of Architects, *Heritage Walk 1*, Council of the City of Chester, 1975

Council of the City of Chester / Chester Society of Architects, *Heritage Walk 2*, Council of the City of Chester, 1977

Council of the City of Chester / Chester Society of Architects, *Heritage Walk 3*, Council of the City of Chester, 1979

Dore, R.N., *Cheshire*, Batsford, 1977

Fenwick, George Lee, *History of Chester*, Phillipson & Golder, 1896

Gelling, Margaret, Nicolaisen, W.F.H. & Richards, Melville, *The Names of Towns & Cities in Britain*, Batsford, 1970

Goulborn, Karlyn & Jackson, Gillian, *Chester: A Portrait In Old Picture Postcards*, SB Publications, 1987

Hollingsworth, Alan, *British Building Styles Recognition*, Town & Country, 1987

Install, Donald W. & Associates, *Chester: A Study in Conservation*, HMSO, 1968

Jarman, C.E., *Chester Cathedral and City*, Jarrold, 1974

Johnson, Paul, *Castles of England, Scotland & Wales*, Weidenfield & Nicolson, 1989

Johnson, Paul, *Cathedrals of England, Scotland & Wales*, Weidenfield & Nicolson, 1990

Kidson, Peter; Murray, Peter; & Thompson, Paul, *A History of English Architecture*, Pelican, 1962

Little, Bryan, *English Cathedrals In Colour*, Batsford, 1972

Mee, Arthur, *The King's England, Cheshire*, Hodder & Stoughton, 1938 revised 1968

Morgan, Kenneth O. (ed.), *The Oxford Illustrated History of Britain*, Oxford University Press, 1984

Pevsner, Nikolaus & Hubbard, Edward, *The Buildings of England, Cheshire*, Penguin, 1971-1990

Rogers, Pat (ed.), Daniel Defoe: *A Tour Through the Whole Island of Great Britain*, 1989

Scott, Rev. S. Cooper, *Lectures on the History of St John Baptist Church and Parish*, Phillipson & Golder, 1892

Sharp, Dennis (ed.), *The Illustrated Dictionary of Architects and Architecture*, Headline, 1991

Simpson, Frank, *Church of St Peter, Chester*, Griffith, 1909

Sugden, Marian & Frankl, Ernest, *Chester*, The Pevensey Press, 1986 revised 1993

Whittington, John, *A Brief History of Chester Station*, Regional Railways North West, 1994

Key to Locations for Walk 1 (Inside The Walls)

1   The High Cross
2   2 Eastgate Street / 1 Bridge Street
3   22 Eastgate Street
4   9-13 Eastgate Street
5   26 Eastgate Street
6   Brown's Crypt Buildings
7   Browns of Chester (38 Eastgate Street)
8   Browns of Chester (34 & 36 Eastgate Street)
9   25 Eastgate Street
10 52 Eastgate Street
11 Grosvenor Precinct
12 Grosvenor Hotel, Eastgate Street
13 Midland Bank, Eastgate Street
14 Barclay's Bank, Eastgate Street
15 Westminster Bank, Eastgate Street
16 St Werburgh Street
17 St Oswald's Chambers, St Werburgh Street
18 Chester Cathedral
19 Former Chapel of St Nicholas, St Werburgh Street
20 St Werburgh Row
21 Barclay's Bank, Northgate Street
22 The Abbey Gateway
23 Abbey Square

24	The Bishop's House
25	The Town Hall, Northgate Street
26	Roman Fragments, Northgate Street
27	City Library, Northgate Street
28	The Odeon, Northgate Street
29	The Pied Bull, Northgate Street
30	The Blue Bell, Northgate Street
31	Shopping Precinct & Indoor Market, Northgate Street
32	Shoemaker's Row, Northgate Street
33	The City Club, Northgate Street
34	St Peter
35	2-4 Bridge Street
36	Deva Hotel, Watergate Street
37	God's Providence House, Watergate Street
38	11 Watergate Street
39	Leche House, Watergate Street
40	Booth Mansions, Watergate Street
41	Bishop Lloyd's House, Watergate Street
42	68 Watergate Street
43	Old Custom House, Watergate Street
44	Guildhall, Watergate Street
45	Stanley Palace, Watergate Street
46	Nicholas Street
47	County Police Headquarters
48	Grosvenor Street
49	St Francis, Grosvenor Street
50	Grosvenor Museum, Grosvenor Street
51	Viking Restaurant, Grosvenor Street
52	The Castle
53	St Mary-on-the-Hill
54	St Mary's Rectory
55	Shipgate House, Shipgate Street
56	Edgar House, Shipgate Street

Key to Locations for Walk 2 (Outside The Walls)

81 Old Bank Buildings, Foregate Street
82 Lloyd's Bank, Foregate Street
83 Blossoms Hotel, Foregate Street
84 Welsh Chapel, St John Street
85 6 St John Street
86 Methodist Church, St John Street
87 The Roman Amphitheatre
88 St John The Baptist
89 The Hermitage, The Groves
90 The Groves
91 Dee Suspension Bridge
92 Grosvenor Park
93 Grosvenor Club, Vicars Lane
94 The Former St John's School, Vicars Lane
95 Forest House, Love Street
96 77 Foregate Street
97 71 Foregate Street
98 Old Queen's Head, Foregate Street
99 Parker's Buildings
100 William Deacon's Bank
101 Bath Street
102 Public Baths, Union Street
103 St Werburgh, Grosvenor Park Road

Key to Locations for Walk 3 (Around The Walls)

Key to Locations for Walk 5 (The North Side)

Key to Locations for Walk 6 (The South Side)

Building for Tomorrow

The Chester Cathedral "Building For Tomorrow" Appeal was launched in May 1995 to raise £2.5 million to fund major development projects:

¤ to open up a new visitors' centre to develop the mission to the one million visitors who visit the Cathedral each year

¤ to replace the badly-worn floor in the Nave and install under-floor heating

¤ to install heating in the South Transept

¤ to improve lighting, amplification and staging to provide concert hall facilities

¤ to rebuild the Monks' Dormitory which was taken down in the last century. The area created will become a new Song School for the Cathedral Choir and allow the development of an Education Centre for the Cathedral, which will be a valuable resource for schools.

Enquires and contributions should be addressed to:

The Chester Cathedral Development Trust
FREPOST (CS1524)
Chester
CH1 2YZ
Tel: 01244 324756
Fax: 01244 341110

Also of interest:

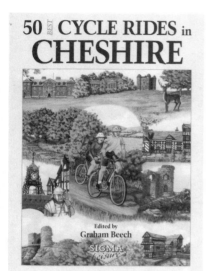

50 BEST CYCLE RIDES IN CHESHIRE

Edited by Graham Beech, this super collection of cycle rides is perfect for family groups or individuals looking for pleasant days in the saddle, without the problems of busy roads. Explore historic villages and interesting towns throughout the county.

"Every cyclist should be leaping into their saddles with this new book" – The Cheshire Magazine

£7.95

TEA SHOP WALKS IN CHESHIRE

Take a pleasant walk in the Cheshire countryside and reward yourself with a leisurely afternoon tea in the county's varied tea shops. A wide range of walks, packed with interest and perfect for everybody who enjoys leisurely walks. *£6.95*

(Other books in our TEASHOP WALKS series cover the Peak District, Lake District, Cotswolds, Devon and Chilterns – all £6.95 each)

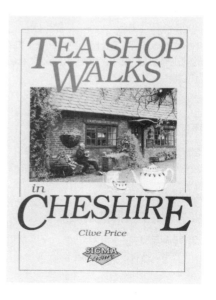

TOWN AND VILLAGE DISCOVERY TRAILS: CHESHIRE

This book is in our new series aimed at walkers planning to explore the best parts of England without taking to the high hills — boots are not required! Visit the best parts of Cheshire and discover the historical heritage of the county

£6·95

Other Books about Cheshire:

BEST PUB WALKS IN & AROUND CHESTER & THE DEE VALLEY

John Haywood explores the historic area based on Chester and Wrexham. Bags of history, superb pubs . *£6.95*

CHESHIRE WALKS WITH CHILDREN

Nick Lambert's book will occupy the whole family. Walks to enjoy, quizzes to answer, things to look for! *£6.95*

PUB WALKS IN CHESHIRE

A well-established book by Jen Darling covering country walks throughout the county with tried and tested pubs to welcome ramblers. *£6.95*

EAST CHESHIRE WALKS

The definitive guidebook, by Graham Beech, to walks in the wilder parts of Cheshire! *£5.95*

WEST CHESHIRE WALKS

Gentle walks by Jen Darling – the perfect companion volume to our East Cheshire title. *£5.95*

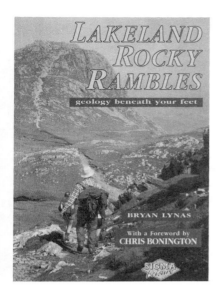

Lake District:

THE LAKELAND SUMMITS – Tim Synge *(£7.95)*

100 LAKE DISTRICT HILL WALKS – Gordon Brown *(£7.95)*

LAKELAND ROCKY RAMBLES: Geology beneath your feet – Brian Lynas *(£9.95)*

FULL DAYS ON THE FELLS: Challenging Walks – Adrian Dixon *(£7.95)*

PUB WALKS IN THE LAKE DISTRICT – Neil Coates *(£6.95)*

LAKELAND WALKING, ON THE LEVEL – Norman Buckley *(£6.95)*

MOSTLY DOWNHILL: LEISURELY WALKS, LAKE DISTRICT – Alan Pears *(£6.95)*

Yorkshire:

YORKSHIRE: A WALK AROUND MY COUNTY – Tony Whittaker *(£7.95)*

YORKSHIRE DALES WALKING: On The Level – Norman Buckley *(£6.95)*

PUB WALKS IN THE YORKSHIRE DALES – Clive Price *(£6.95)*

PUB WALKS ON THE NORTH YORK MOORS & COAST – Stephen Rickerby *(£6.95)*

PUB WALKS IN THE YORKSHIRE WOLDS – Tony Whittaker *(£6.95)*

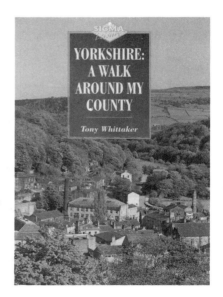

Cycling:

OFF-BEAT CYCLING IN THE PEAK DISTRICT – Clive Smith *(£6.95)*

MORE OFF-BEAT CYCLING IN THE PEAK DISTRICT – Clive Smith *(£6.95)*

CYCLING IN THE LAKE DISTRICT – John Wood *(£7.95)*

CYCLING IN LINCOLNSHIRE – Penny & Bill Howe *(£7.95)*

CYCLING IN NOTTINGHAMSHIRE – Penny & Bill Howe *(£7.95)*

CYCLING IN STAFFORDSHIRE – Linda Wain *(£7.95)*

Cookery:

MILDRED SMITH'S FAVOURITE FAMILY RECIPES

Written by the much-loved star of Granada TV's "The Main Ingredient", this is packed with tempting recipes: everything from a simple (and foolproof) sauce to such treats as sticky tofffee pudding, banoffee pie and other sweets too nice to mention. Vegetarians are not neglected, with tasty recipes that the whole family will enjoy. £6.95.   *And don't miss the companion to this book:*

MILDRED SMITH'S TRADITIONAL RECIPES

– a super collection of easy-to-cook recipes and a perfect introduction to Mildred's homely style of cookery. £4.95.

All of our books are available from your local bookshop. In case of difficulty, or to obtain our complete catalogue, please contact:

Sigma Leisure, 1 South Oak Lane, Wilmslow, Cheshire SK9 6AR
Phone: 01625 – 531035   Fax: 01625 – 536800
E-mail: sigma.press@zetnet.co.uk

ACCESS and VISA orders welcome – call our friendly sales staff or use our 24 hour Answerphone service! Most orders are despatched on the day we receive your order – you could be enjoying our books in just a couple of days. Please add £2 p&p to all orders.